John Webster's sermons are a breath of fresh air—submissive to the biblical text, grounded in Christian doctrine, and focused on God. Webster preached in the conviction that "Christ is the preeminent reality of all things." This basic confession rendered his sermons mercifully free of platitudes and entertainment, instead offering sinners the abundant reality of God's kingdom in Jesus Christ.

HANS BOERSMA
Saint Benedict Servants of Christ Chair in Ascetical Theology,
Nashotah House Theological Seminary

Preaching in Oxford brought out the best in John Webster. Even as his academic theology grew in sophistication, subtlety, and scope, his sermons gave him space to hear and speak the very words of God. By his own admission, his work at Oxford was sometimes overly defensive, but in the pulpit he summoned the confidence to speak of God and the gospel defenselessly. Though these homilies have an elevated tone appropriate for college chapel, Webster's voice here is more direct than allusive, more quotable than cautious, more wise than clever.

FRED SANDERS
Torrey Honors Institute, Biola University

These are truly uplifting sermons. We see in them the work of a master theologian. Deeply edifying in tone, this splendid collection has twenty-seven stellar engagements with the biblical testimony in all its arresting grandeur. Webster was a gifted hearer of the Word. His efforts in proclaiming the incarnate Word warrant careful and scrupulous study.

CHRISTOPHER HOLMES
Head of the Theology Programme, University of Otago

Grace challenges and judges so many of our expectations and presumptions, and it cuts against the grain of our sense that we are masters of our own fates and can self-diagnose our own needs. John Webster helps slow us down to hear the searching, bruising word of the gospel that we might die and be raised anew by Christ. These proclamations hammer against the hardened walls of a too-frequently secularized church, reminding us that Jesus is alive and active, and that we, therefore, have great hope.

MICHAEL ALLEN
John Dyer Trimble Professor of Systematic Theology,
Reformed Theological Seminary

Wonderfully accessible and delightful sermons by a preacher who knew what it meant to speak the gospel and speak it well. Self-effacing, faithful, lucid, and pastoral, these addresses direct us beautifully to the Saviour who presents himself in Holy Scripture. We are here invited to know the one whose reality is "superabundantly real, real above all things," to live and bear witness anew in light of his unfathomably generous goodness.

IVOR J. DAVIDSON
Honorary Research Professor in Divinity,
University of Aberdeen

How wonderful to have these sermons! John Webster's untimely death in 2016 has left his friends and admirers with an enduring grief. But now his incomparable voice is back again in an unexpected form. This treasury of sermons shows John Webster at his best. They are uncommonly solid, sturdy. and no-nonsense expositions full of protein for the soul. Preachers who hope to revitalize and sustain the church would do well to follow Webster's prophetic example.

GEORGE HUNSINGER
Professor of Systematic Theology,
Princeton Theological Seminary

Holy Scripture is meant to be read, proclaimed, prayed, and sung by God's people. Academic study of the sacred page follows from these primary uses and flourishes in serving them. In this collection of homilies, we see the late Professor Webster as a servant of the word's primary use among God's people. These expositions are a gift: faithful to Holy Scripture, brief, clear, and edifying.

SCOTT R. SWAIN
President and James Woodrow Hassell Professor of
Systematic Theology, Reformed Theological Seminary

John Webster's life ended far too early, but what he gave us while he lived is a treasure. Throughout his career he lived and wrote in dedicated service to the good news of Christ, rooted in the conviction that, in and through Holy Scripture, the living Christ speaks to us, here and now. These sermons are a testament to that conviction. In them Webster reiterates, with unadorned simplicity, the gospel attested by the apostles and prophets. Their drumbeat theme is the omnipotent grace of the triune God revealed in the incarnation, passion, and exaltation of Jesus. In him, God is with us, and in these sermons, Webster won't let us forget it.

BRAD EAST
Assistant Professor of Theology, Abilene Christian University

These sermons are erudite; they show the marks of a scholar. But their point can be boiled down to something quite simple that Webster says toward the outset of the collection: "The gospel is true." The truth of the gospel—the truth that Jesus is Savior and Lord—is the word that Webster wants to offer us. And for that we can be grateful to a true theologian.

MATTHEW LEVERING
James N. and Mary D. Perry Jr.
Chair of Theology, Mundelein Seminary

CHRIST

OUR

SALVATION

CHRIST
OUR SALVATION

Expositions and Proclamations

JOHN WEBSTER

EDITED BY DANIEL BUSH

LEXHAM PRESS

Christ Our Salvation: Expositions and Proclamations

Lexham Press, 1313 Commercial St., Bellingham, WA 98225
LexhamPress.com

Print ISBN 9781683594208
Digital ISBN 9781683594215
Library of Congress Control Number 2020941749

Edited by Daniel J. Bush
Lexham Editorial: Abigail Stocker, Kelsey Matthews, Danielle Thevenaz
Cover Design: Micah Ellis
Book Design and Typesetting: Abigail Stocker

CONTENTS

Part III
SALVATION'S HEART

Part IV
SALVATION'S VIRTUES

Part V
PROCLAIMING SALVATION

PREFACE

Those familiar with contemporary preaching are accustomed to the use of narrative and illustrative stories to capture the imagination and keep the big guy in the choir from falling asleep. I admit, I've been under a considerable amount of stress in my own preaching to find the "right" illustration after completing exegesis. John Webster is concerned with story, too, yet it isn't captivating illustrations to provide color commentary that concerns him. In message after message, he maintains laser focus on the gospel story, unfolding in extended paraphrase the narrative of salvation found in holy Scripture.

This, for Webster, is the central task of preaching. The task of preaching isn't to entertain; far less is it to draw attention to the preacher. Rather, the preacher's task is to get out of the way, to let God's own self-revelation through the written and proclaimed word do the work. And if this is to happen, then the word alone must be primary. Guided by conviction concerning the sufficiency and reliability of holy Scripture, Webster takes no liberties but simply preaches. He doesn't speak what is his but speaks only the story of salvation as presented in Scripture. The result is captivating: the hearer (or in this case, the reader) begins to hear the God of Scripture speak, addressing the church with the gospel of salvation.[1]

---

1. John Webster, *Holy Scripture: A Dogmatic Sketch* (New York, NY: Cambridge University Press, 2003), 32.

It was a gray sky afternoon, not uncommon in Aberdeen, when I sat with John in his study at King's College and he entrusted to me the messages that make up this volume. We also discussed at length his preaching. By this I'm not referring to the dogmatics of homiletics but the very human issue of mechanics. When he was called upon to preach, he would read the Scripture passage for the service a few times and prayerfully mull it over. He would check one or two commentaries and perhaps look at what John Owen had said, then he would just write so as to submit himself personally to the rule of holy Scripture, saying again in contemporary speech what had already been said and nothing more. His aim, as he emphatically put it to me, was for listeners to hear what the Spirit—rather than John Webster—says to the church.

The reader should be aware that John's primary audience was within a university environment. The majority of the messages were delivered at Christ Church Cathedral in Oxford where he served as a canon during his tenure as the Lady Margaret Professor of Divinity at Oxford's Christ Church college from 1996–2003. A few messages were delivered at King's College, University of Aberdeen, and elsewhere (see index). The point is that his audience were intellectual and more or less homogeneous, like-minded listeners.

Through the messages assembled in this volume, one thing stands out clearly: Webster was constrained by the Spirit and the rule of Scripture to bear witness before this audience to the "one needful thing" (Luke 10:42). However well he might have felt that he succeeded as a witness is beside the point—honest preachers are notoriously self-deprecating and John was no different—for he was faithful and true to the one who called him. The attentive reader will hear Christ and forget the preacher.

With great honor and heartfelt remembrance, I share these meditations entrusted to me so long ago. Job well done, John!

DANIEL BUSH

CHRIST
OUR SALVATION

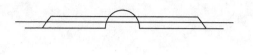

PART I

SOUNDING
SALVATION

I

THE UNFATHOMABLY MIRACULOUS REALITY

"FOR God so loved the world, that he gave his only Son, that whoever believes in him should not perish but have eternal life. For God did not send his Son into the world to condemn the world, but in order that the world might be saved through him."

JOHN 3:16–17

Jesus' encounter with Nicodemus is one of the great resonant passages of the Gospel of John, nowhere more so than in the deep words of John 3:16–17. Of course, they're familiar to many of us, but each time we hear them what strikes us is their capacity to find us out and address us in the vanity and wretchedness of sin.

Whether they're Jesus' words or the words of John the evangelist, we don't know. It doesn't matter too much; what's clear is that in them we have set before us something of the limitless scope and infinite depth of the reality that we call salvation. Here, in this little comment on the gospel story of the Son's saving work, we're told with utter simplicity what we've to do with the gospel—what we've to do with the fact that in Jesus, so well-known and yet so completely different, we face God working the world's salvation. The theme of the gospel is this, simply this and nothing other than this: *that the world might be saved through him.*

In the man Jesus, something has taken place which constitutes an entire renewal of the world, a remaking of reality, a setting aside of a reality ruined beyond repair and the making of something bewilderingly new. That new reality is what we mean by salvation. What may we learn here of this simple and yet unfathomably miraculous reality? Four things we may care to ponder.

First, *the cause of salvation is the love of God.* What lies at the root of the saving ministry of Jesus Christ is God's love. The deep ground of our salvation is this: "God so loved the world" (John 3:16). We must not assume that we know what God's love is, for it is *God's* love—not just a magnified or improved version of the love that we try to practice, but something with its own very particular dignity and glory.

The dignity and glory of God's love is that it's a love which creates and preserves fellowship. God's love is known in his willing and creating of a reality which will be under him and alongside him as the object of his love and mercy. God's love means that he's not only God for himself but God with us and God for us. And in being in this way *our* God, God with us and for us, God binds himself in love to what he has made. His love creates fellowship, creates us to be his. And it also preserves fellowship; it protects what God loves from all the threats to fellowship. God's love is God's resolve, the unshakeable purpose with which God determines that the fellowship that he creates will not be spoiled or overthrown. God's love has a direction, a goal: that the creature whom God loves will flourish, that nothing will finally overcome fellowship—in short, that God will be with us, and we will be with God. God's love creates and preserves us to keep company with him. What we call salvation is caused by nothing other than God's act of love which ensures that this will be so. God loves as Savior; salvation is the love of God in action.

Second, the real quality of the love of God can be seen as we consider the *object of the love of God.* What is it that God loves so much?

The world. And "the world" doesn't just mean the totality of the things which God has made. It means the creation which has rejected God, and, most especially, it means the human creature in rebellion against God—in other words, us. God loves and creates us as objects for his love, human partners for fellowship. We repudiate God: rather than living out of God's love and living for fellowship with God, we seek to be creatures on our own—to be free of what we stupidly think to be the hindrances and obstructions to our freedom that God's love puts in our way.

We do not want fellowship with God; we *will not* have it, and we struggle against it with all our might. We would rather destroy ourselves, and do destroy ourselves, rather than live out of God's love. All this means, therefore, is that God's love isn't set on some worthy object, something which could expect or invite the love of God. God loves the world; God loves us in our contradiction and hatred and renunciation of his love, loves us in all our unloveliness. And so the love of God which is the root of salvation is always and only mercy, pure and simple pity for ruined creatures who have broken fellowship with God.

This loving mercy of God is manifest, third, in the *means of salvation*, which is the coming of the Son of God. How does God save us, his ruined creatures, and restore us to fellowship with him? Not simply by looking upon us with a loving attitude; not simply by a declaration; not simply by offering an example of love. No! God's love is God's act. It's the act of God himself in the persons of the Father and the Son. For, we read, "he gave his only Son"; and again, "God did not send his Son into the world to condemn the world" (John 3:16, 17). Salvation means that God the Father *gives* and *sends* his only Son, and it means that God the Son is given and sent. Salvation isn't a mere word or attitude but a sending and a being sent, a giving and a being given. It's a sending into a giving to *the world*. God enters the realm of our hostility and estrangement. He comes into the very midst of our broken fellowship. That which is utterly unthinkable—that God should still seek to keep faith with his faithless creatures—is what happens in Jesus Christ. In the coming of the Son of God, we're reconciled to God.

We're not reconciled by anything that we ourselves do or could ever do, for the simple reason that there's nothing we can do. The world cannot restore its fellowship with God. We're reconciled to God because God turns to us, and sends his Son, and in sending him gives him to us, and in giving him brings about our salvation.

Which leads, fourth, to the *end or purpose of God's saving work*, which is that we should live. Salvation is God's act that ensures that his purpose of fellowship will be undefeated. This means that God excludes, indeed abolishes, what we fear above all things—perishing, condemnation. "God did not send his Son into the world to condemn"; God sent his Son so that we "should not perish" (John 3:17, 16). Perishing and condemnation, our final fall into death and damnation, have been once and for all excluded by the love of God in Jesus Christ.

There is no condemnation for those in Christ Jesus, literally: death and damnation have ceased to be (Rom 8:1). They've been replaced by a new kind of aliveness, by reconciliation with God, by restored fellowship, by acquittal—in short, by salvation, summed up here in John's Gospel by the words "eternal life."

Eternal life is life in God's company, life under God's mercy, life rooted in God's love. Its origin is in God's mercy; its security is in the love of Christ; its end is the life everlasting. What takes place in Jesus Christ isn't the mere possibility of this life with God, not a mere offer or hope or aspiration, but the very reality of eternal life. In Jesus Christ, God saves not just potentially or in prospect but actually, with all the authority and certainty of God himself.

When we gather week by week, a company of people who get together to hear some words from a book and to eat and drink at a table, the place where we gather is the place of salvation. We're in the domain of salvation. We're in the world which God has loved and reconciled, and we're people whom God has loved and reconciled. What are we to do in response to the miracle of God's saving love? In a very real sense, we're to do *nothing*. We're to do nothing because there is in one sense nothing to do; God has done it all for us. We don't need to try to make salvation happen by moral effort or liturgical performance or having wretched thoughts about our sins. That God loves us and has saved us is as sure as the fact that the sky is blue.

What that reality requires of us is the strange act of faith. The God who loves us and saves us in his Son requires simply that we *believe in him* (John 3:16). To believe in him is not to add our bit to the work of salvation, clinching the deal by signing on the dotted line. If we think that, we're saying that we're saved by our faith, not by God. Faith lets God do God's work. Faith rests in the fact that from all eternity God is our God and he has pledged himself to us finally in sending his Son, giving him to us that we may not perish but have life with God. "For God did not send his Son into the world to condemn the world, but in order that the world might be saved through him" (John 3:17). Whoever believes in him is not condemned.

May God give us joy and trust in these things. Amen.

II

A REAWAKENED AFFECTION

Oʜ how I love your law!
   It is my meditation all the day.
Your commandment makes me wiser than my enemies,
   for it is ever with me.
I have more understanding than all my teachers,
   for your testimonies are my meditation.
I understand more than the aged,
   for I keep your precepts.
I hold back my feet from every evil way,
   in order to keep your word.
I do not turn aside from your rules,
   for you have taught me.
How sweet are your words to my taste,
   sweeter than honey to my mouth!
Through your precepts I get understanding;
   therefore I hate every false way.

PSALM 119:97–104

One of the most weighty claims that the Christian gospel makes on human life is the reordering of our affections. That is, faith in Jesus Christ and life lived under his governance requires not only a change in our practices, ideas, and attitudes but a deeper alteration, one which underlies those things. That deeper change is a change in what we *love*. If the gospel is indeed to take up residence in us, it can only do so as our affections are transformed and our hearts are set on new things. Until that happens—until our affections are made new by being set on new objects—the work of regeneration will remain incomplete.

Why the affections? What makes them of such cardinal importance in the life of Christian discipleship? Often in common speech we use the word "affection" to mean a not-very-passionate liking for something: we talk of an affection for cats and dogs, or antiques—something nice and possibly absorbing yet hardly earth-shattering. But affection can also be used in a deeper sense to indicate the fundamental loves which govern us and determine the shape of our lives. In particular, the affections are that part of us through which we attach ourselves to things outside of ourselves. Sometimes the object of our affections may be a person, or a form of activity, or a set of ideas; whatever it is, we cleave to it through the affections. When we set our affections on something, we come to regard it as supremely significant, valuable, and praiseworthy. It offers us a satisfaction and fulfillment which we cannot derive from other things, and we arrange our lives in such a way that we take every opportunity to enjoy that satisfaction and experience that fulfillment. In this way, our affections—our loves, which are fixed on certain realities, and our desires, which long for what we love—are one of the driving forces of our lives. The affections are in a real sense the engines of our attitudes and actions. What we are and what we do cannot be separated from what we love.

Because the affections are so important, the consequences of human sin upon the affections are particularly catastrophic. Sin means alienation from God, and alienation from God means the detachment of the affections from their proper objects. Our desiring and loving become disordered. We attach ourselves to the wrong things; we come to take satisfaction and fulfillment not from what God has ordained as the means of our flourishing but from wicked things. No longer a means of adhering to our good, no longer a way of cleaving to God's ways for us, our affections are detached from God. Our affections no longer follow the truth; they become chaotic; they are a sign of the breakdown of our lives as creatures.

This disintegration of the affections as they lose their grip on the truth is no slight business; it is one of the greatest signs of our human degeneracy, and no amount of human effort can heal us. If the affections are to be renewed and the disorder overcome, it can only be by a work of God that makes human life new. That is, the affections can only be renewed by baptism. They must submit to that twofold work of God in which we are put to death and raised from the dead. Like everything else about us, the affections must be judged and condemned, exposed in all their falsehood and malice and vanity, and they must be recreated by the power of God's Spirit.

If we are to be disciples of Jesus Christ, our affections must be put to death. Attachments have to be broken; our love must be separated from its false objects; we must learn to abhor and turn from the things to which our disorderly affections cling. That process, the putting to death of false affections, is no slight work of a moment; it is a long, hard effort, one in which we have to fight ourselves and our circumstances. We hang on like limpets to the objects of our affections. We fear losing the things to which we cling, even when we know they are destructive, because we cannot believe that there is any good for us without them, and so dying to such false affections is the work of a lifetime as we try to deny ourselves and inch forward toward holiness. But the putting to death of the affections is only the reverse side of their being remade. As we grow in holiness, our affections are not destroyed; rather, they are attached to fitting objects as we learn to love and desire the right things. Moving ahead in the Christian life depends a great deal upon this reordering of our affections. Experiences, moral effort, religious exercises will not get us very far unless the affections are engaged and we are drawn away from unworthy loves to our true end.

Now, all that is a prologue to coming to terms with something Psalm 119 works to hammer into our souls—namely, that one of the hallmarks of the spiritual life is a reawakened affection for God and the ways of God. One of the chief fruits of our remaking by the Holy Spirit is a delight in God's law. "Oh, how I love your law!" Or again: "How sweet are your words to my taste, sweeter than honey to my mouth!" (Ps 119:97, 103). What does the psalmist mean here by God's "law"?

We're schooled by our culture to think that nothing could be less delightful than law. Law instinctively seems to be something arbitrary and inhibiting. For the psalmist, however, law is an altogether wholesome and delightful matter.

God's law is not an arbitrary set of statutes managed by some divine magistrate; still less is it a mechanism for relating to God through a system of rewards for good conduct and punishments for misbehavior. God's law is best thought of as God's personal presence. It is God's gift of himself, in which he comes to his people in fellowship and sets before them his will for human life. God's law is the claim that God makes upon us as our Maker and Redeemer. And because it is *his* claim—the claim of the one who made us and has redeemed us—God's law calls us to be what we have been made and redeemed to be: God's people, those who are to live with him and for him and so find fulfillment and peace.

The law which is celebrated all through Psalm 119 is our vocation to be human; it is the form of life with God, the path of real human flourishing. And that is why it engages our affections and fills us with delight. "How sweet are your words to my taste, sweeter than honey to my mouth!" (Ps 119:103). When the affections are converted back to God, then God's law ceases to be a threat; it's no longer something we merely respect or fear. We're not terrified of it like slaves, and our keeping of it is not craven, sullen, inhibited adherence to rules. It is delightful: we enjoy its sweetness because we know God's law isn't a prison but a space in which we can grow and thrive.

We can learn a good deal about ourselves if we inquire into our lives from this angle. If we're alert and conscientious Christian people and not lazy or couldn't-care-less about our faith, then we'll want to examine ourselves now and again—to try to be aware of what we're up to, how things stand with us in this great matter of our fellowship with God. Self-examination shouldn't, of course, be overscrupulous or anxious; it shouldn't drive us inside ourselves or make us feel defeated by our muddles. It should always be rooted in the assurance that God is much better at forgiving us than we are at forgiving ourselves. But, with those things in mind, the wise Christian will, from time to time, want to ask: Where do my affections lie? If I am as truthful as I can be about myself, what draws my desires? What are the objects of my loving? When I look dispassionately and without illusion at who I am, what is the substance of my delights? As we engage in that kind of reflection and try, as it were, to take the temperature of our spiritual lives, the psalm offers us two tests, two lines of inquiry to help us see our lives in the light of the truth. Both of them are ways of asking how deeply our affections are engaged by the law of God and how firm our attachment is to his ways for humankind.

The first test is this: *affection for God's law will be demonstrated in spiritual meditation.* "Oh how I love your law! It is my meditation all the day" (Ps 119:97). Those whose affections delight in God's law will spend a great deal of time pondering it. Why? Because sin confuses our thinking. It makes us unsteady and unstable; it distracts us by filling our minds with a great clutter of falsehoods, and those falsehoods prevent us from seeing the truth and setting our affections on the truth.

Sin makes sure that we can't see the truth and so can't love it. But as the Spirit takes hold of us and makes us new, one of the things brought about is a new focusing of our lives. We become more centered; our lives and our affections are directed to the simple and utterly attractive reality of God. And when our affections are set on God, then our minds follow: we begin to meditate on God and God's law, and God's ways with us become the sub-stance of our thoughts.

Of course, the meditation which the psalmist is talking about here isn't unfocused reverie, the free play of our religious feelings. It's something very specific, very distinctive. It's attention to God's law in which God manifests himself and his will for human life. It's what happens when the law of God so fills our hearts, minds, and wills that it becomes the lens through which we see every-thing, the norm which we consult in order to figure out what we are to be and do. For the person whose affections are set on God, that kind of meditation is the default setting of our minds; it's what we keep returning to because, as the psalmist puts it, "Your commandment makes me wiser than my enemies, for it is ever with me" (Ps 119:98).

This isn't a matter for pride. Quite the reverse: it means that we do not think of ourselves as the masters of wisdom for living but that we simply ponder God's instruction, knowing that what we know is what we're taught by God. Nor is it a matter of theory alone. Meditation isn't abstract, merely entertaining right notions; it's searching God's law in order to be instructed in the way we should live. "Through your precepts I get understand-ing," the psalmist says—that is, practical wisdom for framing my life (Ps 119:104). God's law tells us that God is *this* God, that his ways with us are *these* ways, and that we are called to act in their light. So to meditate on God is to find guidance, direction, a shape for our living.

The second test is this: *affection for God's law will be demon-strated in avoidance of wickedness.* "I hold back my feet from every evil way, in order to keep your word. ... Through your precepts I get understanding; therefore I hate every false way" (Ps 119:101, 104). Corresponding to our turning toward God in practical meditation on the law of God is a turning away from what stands opposed to God's ways.

As our lives are made new by God's Spirit, our affections are set on God's law; that law gives us understanding, and that understanding in turn enables *discrimination*. That is, we begin to see what is good and what is evil and to embrace the will of God. That embracing of the will of God involves us in making a very clear refusal. It means keeping our feet from evil paths, not departing from God's laws. It means we have to say no to ourselves. It means we have to stop thinking of our lives as a sort of empty space to fill as we wish and instead see that we're directed to walk in a very specific direction, and only in that direction.

But we can only do that if our desire for wickedness is supplanted by a desire for God, because desire for God will inevitably generate an aversion to what's excluded by God's law. That aversion is to be real and strong: "I hate every false way," the psalmist says (Ps 119:104). A kind of singleness in our affections is commanded of us; vacillation, commitment to both sides, is simply not possible. Purity of heart means to will one thing and one thing only, which is the will of God that is set before us in his law and to which, by God's Spirit, our affections are attached.

We've only just scratched the surface of this magnificent bit of Holy Scripture; there is enough here to give us the matter for much thought and prayer. To help us on our way, here's a prayer of Miles Coverdale, the sixteenth-century bishop of Exeter:

> O Lord Jesus Christ, draw thou our hearts unto thee; join them together in inseparable love, that we may ever abide in thee and thou in us, and that the everlasting covenant between us may stand sure for ever. Let the fiery darts of thy love pierce through all our slothful members and inward powers, that we, being happily wounded, may so become whole and sound. Let us have no lover but thyself alone; let us seek no joy and comfort except in thee; for thy name's sake. Amen.

III

HE HAS SET US FREE

AND he said to them, "Well did Isaiah prophesy of you hypocrites, as it is written,

'This people honors me with their lips,
    but their heart is far from me;
in vain do they worship me,
    teaching as doctrines the commandments of men.'

You leave the commandment of God and hold to the tradition of men."

MARK 7:6–8

Conflict is a common discourse in the holy Scriptures, especially in the Gospel narratives. In his Gospel, Mark zooms in on a localized conflict, catching in his lens a bitter dispute about tradition. The laws of ritual cleansing that were such a given in the religious world of early Christianity are the issue of the hour: "Why do your disciples not walk according to the tradition of the elders, but eat with defiled hands?" ask the Pharisees and the scribes (Mark 7:5). There is outrage in the question.

This isn't merely the kind of outrage with which we naturally treat our competitors as we try to expose them as the frauds they are, but something deeper. It's outrage about the fact that Jesus threatens something absolutely basic to the posture of the people of God in the world. What he seems to be threatening is holiness,

13

separation. He seems to be just striding over all the boundaries that had been so carefully erected and which were so carefully patrolled because they marked the distinction between the people of God and the pagan occupier. The rites of cleansing which surrounded eating and drinking were not just bits of religious ornamentation; they were ways of giving tangible expression to the fact that God's people wouldn't compromise their elect status, wouldn't pollute themselves and become like the gentiles. What's at stake, therefore, is the very identity of God's people, their distinctiveness, the visibility of their difference, and, in the end, the obedience due to the Lord of the covenant. Jesus' very casualness about ritual matters isn't just disrespectful to the elders; it strikes at the heart of how the people of God ought to be the people of God.

Or at least, that's the theory. For Jesus, there's just as much at stake as for his opponents. His opposition to them isn't merely a matter of recommending a more relaxed, unfussy attitude, less scrupulous and therefore less likely to get things out of proportion. No, for Jesus—as for his opponents—what's at stake is the radical demand that the law of God makes on the people of God. Far from seeking to loosen up the law and soften its force, Jesus is urging that his opponents have missed the point. In establishing a set of regulations to embody commitment to God's law, he claims that his opponents have set the whole law aside. Their problem, therefore, isn't over-obedience; it's faithlessness. It's a faithlessness that manifests itself as scruple, but faithlessness it is, and Jesus is unsparing in exposing it to judgment.

What's gone wrong? At its heart, this: *tradition has inserted itself between the people of God and the Lord of their lives.* "You leave the commandment of God and hold to the tradition of men" (Mark 7:8). It's important to realize the problem isn't tradition itself. In and of itself, tradition is both innocent and, indeed, positively helpful. Traditions are orderly ways of living human life, ways of living that work with given, inherited values and try to negotiate all sorts of human situations with the resources that those inherited values offer. The great strength of tradition is that it refuses to believe that in every situation we have to start afresh—that we never have anything to learn from the accumulated wisdom of the past. To live in tradition is to live a life with a shape that I don't just make up as I go along but which comes from before me, which gives me a shape, which helps me make sense of the world, and which puts me in touch with resources that I can't just pull out of my own stores.

People often lament the lack of traditions in a good deal of modern life, and there's a truth in the lament. The need for roots is something very deep in us; the lack of roots is very destructive. It's destructive above all when we're faced with challenges from new situations. Wise communities take stock of their situations by looking to their past and trying to figure out from that vantage point what they're called to do. One thing we might pray for is that our own bit of Christianity may be given grace to think about its traditions before it catapults itself into the future like some kind of unguided missile.

But for all the good things that tradition brings, it can also turn against us. It can become not the shape of our lives but a straitjacket; not a role to play but a shell to hide in. Tradition can become God's enemy and our own. How does this happen?

Tradition works well when it's a response to a call. A healthy and effective tradition is one that offers a way of living our lives in responsibility, in answer to a summons from outside ourselves to be a particular kind of people. What a tradition does is help us find ways of building our lives around that summons and of making sure that the summons is always laid before us. In the Christian tradition, for example, creeds and set forms of prayer serve just this need: They help us focus; they help us fix mind and heart and will and imagination on the particular reality of the gospel; they prevent us from drifting into formlessness; they shape our lives into an answer to the call of God in Christ. But religious traditions in particular go wrong when, instead of giving access to the call of God, they become a substitute for it. The tradition somehow freezes; it interposes itself between God and the people of God; obedience to God becomes submission to the tradition. Then, we might say, tradition is no longer an open window but a closed room. And it's just this corruption of tradition which Jesus uncovers in the little conflict story in Mark 7.

The Pharisees challenge the laxity of Jesus' disciples and thereby challenge Jesus himself. He responds by turning the accusation around and claiming the true fulfillment of the law for himself. His opponents, he says, honor God with their lips but not their hearts. It's a familiar theme in the great prophetic writings of the Old Testament: that ritual is no real substitute for moral obedience; that mercy, not sacrifice, is the fulfillment of the will of God; that cleanliness is of the heart, not the hands. All this lies behind the latter part of the story, where Jesus points to what's already within us as what really poisons the soul.

"For from within, out of the heart of man, come evil thoughts, sexual immorality, theft, murder, adultery, coveting, wickedness, deceit, sensuality, envy, slander, pride, foolishness" (Mark 7:21–22). Wickedness isn't contagious, nor is it something that happens to us as an unfortunate fate imposed from outside. It's who we are. It's the inmost core of ourselves, and no amount of observance of rites, no amount of scrupulous religion and morals, can cover it up, let alone cure us of it. To think that it can is to be what Jesus calls a "hypocrite"—not just someone claiming to be something they aren't, but someone living a lie, someone who can't see the radical inconsistency in their life and who thereby condemns themselves before the judgment of God.

But there's more than hypocrisy here. There's the setting aside of the law of God. The final twist of Jesus' reply to his attackers is that their very scruples, the rigidity of their observances, is an assault on the law of God. They teach as doctrines the precepts of men, and so leave the commandment of God. These "precepts" are the whole assemblage of oral traditions which had built up around the Law of God—a great penumbra of commentary and application of the written Law. The point of the whole edifice was properly to press home the logic of the law in every situation, to bring the totality of human life under obedience to God, to prevent the people of God from thinking that they're ever off the hook, no longer walking in the light of the Lord. But the whole thing, says Jesus, has become a curse and a sin.

It's become not a means of obedience but a means of manipulation; a means of making obedience to God into something that can be measured out and quantified, by which we can congratulate ourselves on having done exactly what God requires. The demands of God thereby become something within our grasp. Those demands don't open us up to God's reality so much as place God in our control. We know what he wants, we do it, and we are satisfied, and so, we think, is God. So we think. But in fact, we've not even begun to obey, because we've tried to have God's commands on our terms. We've tried to make use of the law in such a way that it's muffled: it can no longer tell us the one thing that above all it must tell us—that we're sinners, that we need the mercy of God, that no amount of correct performance can set a sinner free. "Their heart is far from me; in vain do they worship me" (Mark 7:6–7).

Here, I believe, we're told something that is pretty near the heart of the Christian gospel, which is this: *no amount of observance, no amount of carefully monitored religious performance, can give us the right to look God in the face.* Anything that claims to be able to do that for us—traditions, rituals, experiences, dogmas, or anything else—is just a delusion, and, worse still, a kind of pride. It's just another expression of the terrible sin exposed in Jesus' words from Isaiah: "Their hearts are far from me" (Isa 29:13).

What, then, may we hope for? Where may we look for help? The natural temptation of all of us is to think that if God asks us for our hearts we should offer them unreservedly, working with all diligence to make a pure offering of ourselves, thorough, unblemished, without reserve. But in the light of the passage before us, that is to miss the point. The point is not that we're required to do more, to be more diligent and scrupulous, somehow bringing order to our inner demons by ourselves. We're not required to do that, because we can't do that. We can't tame the demon within. The more we try to do so, the more power we give to him, and the more we're enslaved. What's required of us is *nothing*! Which is to say: what is required of us is *faith*.

What is required of us is faith that God has already done for us what we cannot and must not do for ourselves. He has made us into his people. He has established righteousness. He has worked obedience. He has done all this in his Son. And because he has done this, he has set us free. He has set us free from the gnawing anxiety of having to perform, having to be responsible for our own purity. He has set us free, therefore, to discover glad and cheerful obedience. And that is why we are to pray thus:

> Lord of all power and might, who art the author and giver
> of all good things; graft in our hearts the love of thy name,
> increase in us true religion, and of thy great mercy, keep us
> in the same, through Jesus Christ our Lord, Amen.

IV

TRUTH KNOWN
AND LOVED

BLESSED are those whose way is blameless,
　　who walk in the law of the LORD!
Blessed are those who keep his testimonies,
　　who seek him with their whole heart,
who also do no wrong,
　　but walk in his ways!
You have commanded your precepts
　　to be kept diligently.
Oh that my ways may be steadfast
　　in keeping your statutes!
Then I shall not be put to shame,
　　having my eyes fixed on all your commandments.
I will praise you with an upright heart,
　　when I learn your righteous rules.
I will keep your statutes;
　　do not utterly forsake me!
How can a young man keep his way pure?
　　By guarding it according to your word.
With my whole heart I seek you;
　　let me not wander from your commandments!
I have stored up your word in my heart,
　　that I might not sin against you.
Blessed are you, O LORD;
　　teach me your statutes!

With my lips I declare
all the rules of your mouth.
In the way of your testimonies I delight
as much as in all riches.
I will meditate on your precepts
and fix my eyes on your ways.
I will delight in your statutes;
I will not forget your word.

PSALM 119:1–16

Psalm 119 is one long meditation upon human life in relation to God. It's a probing but tender exploration of what human life looks like when it is encountered and caught up by God and God's presence. Above all, it's an attempt to make sense of what happens to us when we come to see that our lives are faced squarely by the fact of God's law—by the fact, as our selection puts it, that it is in "the law of the Lord" that we are to "walk" (Ps 119:1). Taken as a whole, the psalm is an anatomy of life enclosed and addressed and nourished by the law of God, a portrait of the lives and sufferings and consolations of those for whom the law of God is the way along which they must go.

It's pretty hard for us, of course, to think that God's law is our path through life, that law might nourish us, feed our souls. The word "law" has for us a rather juridical and perhaps even hostile or threatening tone. We tend instinctively to think of the law as a body of formal precepts, as something which *rules* us. At worst we can think of it as a domineering, tyrannical demon. And so law scarcely seems the seedbed of human flourishing; rather, it seems something from which we have to escape, something beyond which we have to go if we're to find authenticity and maturity in relation to God and the world.

For Psalm 119, however, law is an altogether more expansive, edifying, and delightful reality. It isn't a set of constraints; it isn't a cage; it isn't a statute book. God's law is—put at its simplest—God's communicative presence. It's God's word—that is, God with us, God coming to us, God establishing fellowship with us, and in that fellowship making himself known, trusted, and loved.

God's law is not first and foremost a code, a set of observable requirements. It's God's revealed presence, God's self-exposition. In his law, God expounds himself, sets himself before us as God who wills to be with us and we with him. And as God sets himself before us in this way, declaring his character in his dealings with us, God also sets before us the normative shape for human life. He expounds what it means to be and act humanly.

His law is his word, his manifestation of himself. But God's eloquence is also God's command. It isn't an alien command; it isn't arbitrary, a matter merely of God's will as a superior power opposed to us that crushes our will and robs our liberty. The command of God's law is simply God setting before us the given shape, the order—the *good* order—of human life in and with God, who makes and saves us. God's law is a *summons*: a summons to be what we're chosen by God to be. God's law forms us; it indicates to us that, if we're to be what we're made to be, then we must be and act in this way.

The point of all this is to try to say that God's law is not just a graceless source of obligation. It's a good gift, something which leads to joy, blessing, and praise. Properly speaking, law is about the fact that God comes to his people with his own kind of merciful majesty, showing us what we must be if we are to be truly human, setting the law between us and our limitless capacity for self-destruction. God's law is God interposing himself between us and our headlong rush into self-destruction, God nurturing us by educating us into the true form of human flourishing. If we would be, and if we would flourish, this is what it means to live joyfully from, with, and under God.

Because all this is true, we can readily see why in the psalm, God's law engages not just the will but the understanding and the affections. It addresses itself to the understanding. That doesn't at all mean that it is a purely intellectual matter, if by that we mean something speculative or abstract and unrelated to the business of living life. It does mean that through the law of God we come to see what really is true about human life and how we're to live in the light of that truth. God's law introduces us to reality; it's about the fact that if life is to work out for us, we have to order our lives in the light of truth. And so God's law brings light; it quickens us by enabling us to see beyond the fretful darkness of sin and learn how to be truthful human beings.

Moreover, God's law addresses itself to the affections. That is, it presents itself as truth to be known *and therefore loved*. The picture of human wisdom and maturity here is a picture of the redeemed heart—of human love snatched back from vanity and fruitless longing and turned back to God, and therefore turned back to the real way in which we can live in fulfillment. Because God's law is nothing other than the loving God pointing us to our fulfillment, the law isn't a source of terror. Quite the opposite: we delight in the law. "In the way of your testimonies I delight as much as in all riches. … I will delight in your statutes; I will not forget your word" (Ps 119:14, 16).

So much, then, for this notion of the law of God—God's word, which addresses us; God's command, which sets us on the way to life. Such a picture of human life is, I fear, scarcely conceivable for most of us, to say nothing of whether we think it livable. The idea that the psalm presupposes—that we live within a given order of reality, that God speaks to us and shapes our lives—is pretty remote to the way most of us go about our day-to-day affairs. Why is that? Largely, I think, because we've inherited a set of cultural conventions that tells us that what's basic in human life is not *hearing* but *willing*. One of the deepest assumptions of our culture is that we've no given nature. We're what we make of ourselves, not what God makes of us or intends for us. There's no creator worth speaking of—no providence, no moral order, no structure to being human. What there is, is our will. We're creatures of our own willing, and in morals and education and politics and medicine and friendship and everything else, what matters is technology, making, producing ourselves. As we make ourselves, so we are.

Within such a culture, the idea of God's law is well outside our field of vision. At the very least, grasping what it's about will involve some seismic shifts in the way we think about ourselves and our world. More than anything, taking this psalm seriously will involve the conversion of the imaginations of our hearts. People can only resist when what they have deep inside them is something so utterly good and true that resistance is worthwhile. The wisdom of the psalm is that God's law is, indeed, utterly good and utterly true and that it can set us free to be and do more than our culture will allow. God's law liberates. That is, once we come to see that there is a shape to our lives that is not what we invent but what God gives to us, we can lay down the burden of having to make ourselves and become what we are: the creatures of the mercy of God.

What might be involved in that? How do we need to have heart and mind converted? Three things from our portion of Psalm 119.

First: *we need to learn to seek God wholeheartedly.* "Blessed are those who keep his testimonies, who seek him with their whole heart," says the psalmist, "With my whole heart I seek you" (Ps 119:10). What's involved in this wholehearted seeking? "Seeking God" doesn't mean looking for something that is lost or hidden from us; rather, it means turning the entirety of one's life toward the one who is present to us, the one whom we can seek because he has already sought and found us. And our seeking of this God involves both a no and a yes. Negatively, it means struggling to retain focus in our lives so that we do not get distracted from the one thing which is really necessary for us. "Let me not wander from your commandments!" (Ps 119:10). If we are truly to seek God, we have to get beyond the aimlessness and instability which so often curses us; we have to reject the endless diversions from concentration upon the ways of God. Positively, we have to make God our aim: to turn to God with a focused intensity because God is the chief and most pressing business of our lives. In everything, we're to be directed toward God and by God. The psalm speaks of having the eyes fixed on all God's commandments, of fixing the eyes on God's ways (Ps 119:6, 15).

What's meant is a setting of the whole person on God as our beginning, way, and end. The will and affections, the mind and desires of the heart, need to be turned to God as our supreme fulfillment, as the end of what it means to be human. And this means a certain steadfastness; the long haul of determining that we will delight in God's statues and will not forget his word (Ps 119:16).

Second, *we need to learn,* as the psalmist tells us, *to "meditate on [God's] precepts"* (Ps 119:15). This meditation, this pondering of God's revealed will for us, is not introspection; it is not anxious, scrupulous self-examination or the cultivation of inner states. It isn't a move inward but a move outward, a pondering that is a listening to what comes to us from God. What the psalmist calls storing up God's word in our heart (Ps 119:11) means exactly that: not governing our lives by what our hearts, consciences, minds, or desires tell us, but letting them be governed by God's word. For Christian people, this means, at its most basic, governing our lives by holy Scripture: letting this collection of texts address us, form us, judge us, and encourage us, and so grow in knowing and keeping God's commandments.

Third, and lastly, *we need to let God do his work in us by his Spirit and change our affections.* We need to submit to the process in which God educates our appetites and desires and trains us to love what he commands. "I will delight in your statutes," the psalmist says (Ps 119:16). The conversion of our desires is what transforms obligation into delight. Converting desires is the office of the Spirit. The work of the Spirit in this matter is usually slow, steady, and undramatic. It happens as the Spirit makes use of the means of grace to knock us into shape and refine us. It happens, therefore, as we listen to the Bible, as we feed on the sacrament, as we try to pray, as we find ourselves set in fellowship with all those others to whom God has shown his law. God uses those things to make us new, to soften our stubbornness and refine our spiritual coarseness into affection for the truth of God.

This, of course, is why the heart of the matter is prayer. Psalm 119 as a whole is one long prayer to God, one long reaching out in need and supplication to God. The core of that prayer is: "Do not utterly forsake me!" (Ps 119:8). We get in the way of God's work in us; we're deaf to what he says and blind to what he shows; we lack eagerness, love, and desire. In and of ourselves we can do nothing to change our situation; in the things of God, we're as weak as kittens. But God is not weak. He will undertake for us. And that is why we pray to God's Spirit that he will do for us what we cannot do for ourselves: that he will not forsake us but quicken us, engage us, and make us alive. Amen.

V

REMEMBERING
OUR PEACE

HE shall judge between the nations,
  and shall decide disputes for many peoples;
and they shall beat their swords into plowshares,
  and their spears into pruning hooks;
nation shall not lift up sword against nation,
  neither shall they learn war anymore.

ISAIAH 2:4

Isaiah's startling prophecy sets before us a picture of God as judge. God is the Lord of the nations, enthroned in a high place yet in the midst of human history, deciding the cause of humanity. Though its words are probably familiar to us, it sets before us something that we likely find hard to accept. Why so?

It's not simply that the idea of God as judge evokes all manner of dreadful pictures of God as accuser, a sort of celestial senior proctor who doles out punishments for crimes. Even when we get ourselves out of those false pictures of God, there's a deeper problem here, which we can describe as something like this. To realize that God is judge strikes at the heart of something which we hold very dear about ourselves. To grasp that it is God who judges is to be dispossessed of our claim to be, ourselves, judges in our own cause. For the entire thrust of what Isaiah has to tell us here is that it is from God, not from we ourselves, that true judgment comes;

he and he alone is the one who utters the final, definitive, and authoritative statement of the truth about our human condition.

Why is this so disturbing to us? Why is it that when we face the claim of God to be our judge we almost inevitably experience a certain resentment?

We resist the judgment of God because we're sinners who prefer to judge ourselves. Part of our human lostness is that we enthrone ourselves as judges. We take upon ourselves the role of deciding between good and evil. We think of ourselves individually or of our group as the norm by which truth is to be decided. It's as if truth and falsehood, right and wrong, are mine, or ours, to decide. I am no longer under judgment; no longer do I submit to a statement of the truth, which is spoken to me from outside. Instead, I myself become the truth, the measure; I come to believe in my own competence. I put myself in the fatal position of believing that I can speak the truth to myself and, above all, to others. And the truth is that I am right, and good, and clean, and others are not.

It is, indeed, a fatal position we put ourselves in, for when this happens, the result is nearly always violence. When I think of myself as competent to judge, then it is as if I want to fill the world with myself and so must push away everything and everyone that poses a threat to me. Once I decide that true judgment is simply what I think, then everything that doesn't fit is seen to be deficient and therefore something that has to be got out of the way.

We know readily enough how this happens in public and political life; our recent history is littered with examples of racial and ethnic conflict that are in large part the dreadful consequences of some group deciding that it is entitled to judge and crush its neighbor. But we see it on a more domestic scale also, in the vigor with which we defend our territory in the workplace, or the family, or in marriage, or in church. When we allow ourselves to believe that we are our own judges, when we think we may speak the truth to ourselves, then conflicts are solved by swords and spears.

It's especially important on Remembrance Sunday[1] to remind ourselves that the conduct of war is caught up within this aspect of human fallenness. This does not mean that the waging of war is always wrong—though it's rarely right in the way in which we suppose it to be. Nor does it mean that we have to slight the extraordinary price paid by so many people, then and now, to restrain evil and defend the peace and order of human society. What it does mean is this: war is just only when it is a repetition of *God's* judgment on evil. War is a just act when it testifies to *God's* condemnation of sin and disorder.

In just war we do not fight for our bit of territory—our cause against our enemies'. War is just only when it upholds *God's* order, *God's* righteousness, when it seeks to repeat and honor the truth of God. And that is why we have to think of war with fear and trembling, as a terrible necessity to which we may be called. To think otherwise—to make war into an occasion for the glorious assertion of our political or technological superiority—is in the end to confuse God's judgment with our own.

It's from that literally fatal confusion that Isaiah's prophecy seeks to deliver us. "It shall come to pass in the latter days that the mountain of the house of the LORD shall be established as the highest of the mountains, and shall be lifted up above the hills; and all the nations shall flow to it" (Isa 2:2). Isaiah sets before us a vision of the future at whose heart is the presence, the overwhelming presence, of the Lord God with his people. He himself, Isaiah tells us, will be with us, enthroned, exalted, raised above the hills, the unmistakable focus of the worship of all humanity. And his presence will entirely eclipse all merely human judging, all merely human decisions about right and wrong, for his presence will be the presence of true judgment, the singular manifestation of the truth: "For out of Zion shall go forth the law, and the word of the LORD from Jerusalem" (Isa 2:3).

---

1. Britain's Memorial Day.

His presence will mean *the* law, *the* order in which human life can flourish; he will speak *the* word, he will lay bare once and for all the truth of human life and history. "He shall judge between the nations, and shall decide disputes for many peoples" (Isa 2:4). Because all this will be so, Isaiah tells us, because of this universal declaration of the righteous judgment of God, then two things will be. There will, first of all, be an end of human division—for God's righteous presence will attract all nations to itself, flowing to its sheer attractiveness and goodness. "Many peoples shall come, and say: 'Come, let us go up to the mountain of the LORD, to the house of the God of Jacob, that he may teach us his ways and that we may walk in his paths' " (Isa 2:3). Second, there will be an end to human violence: the weapons of war will simply be made redundant by the judgment of God.

It may be an attractive enough picture, we may say, but surely utopian, very far from our experience of what the world is really like. The long litany of wars, small and large, in the last decade surely shows that this kind of thing is just a remote hope well over the horizon. What hope for Chechnya, or East Timor, or a dozen other wounded places?

For Christian people, however, these latter days have in one very real sense already come. We live in them. In one very real sense, the establishing of God's judgment has already taken place. And it's taken place in Jerusalem, though not in the temple, but in a far darker place: on a hill outside the gate of the holy city, in the dying of the man Jesus. For it is in him that God's final judgment is declared and becomes finally effective. There, God's truth is manifest; there, sin and death are robbed of their power to destroy. For he, Jesus Christ, is God's law; he is God's Word; he, the one judged and sent to death is himself the Judge of all things, and in him alone we and all other poor sinners are to find our peace.

In the end, this means that war and all the sheer waste and wretchedness of war stand under something else: the judgment of God, which Ephesians calls "the gospel of peace" (Eph 6:15). The gospel of peace isn't some misty-eyed and wholly unrealistic dream of a world without conflict. It's a declaration—*God's* declaration—that in Jesus Christ, peace *is*, because Jesus Christ *is*. He is our peace. It's in and as him that God makes wars to cease.

Therefore, today, we're called to do two things. We're called, first of all, to remember. We remember with gratitude and no doubt with some heaviness those who have found themselves caught up in human conflict and have tried to witness to God's good order for human life. But more, we remember one who was himself led like a lamb to the slaughter, one who by oppression and judgment was taken away, and one who above all has made many to be accounted righteous.

It's the task of the Christian church, of all Christian people, to work together on forms of life that do that kind of remembering: very simply, to live our lives with a vivid awareness of Jesus, a vivid remembering of the fact that by his life, death, and resurrection, he has turned the world upside down. Such remembering is crucial to making sure that we aren't trapped into thinking that the present is all that there is, that violence can't end: for we remember that the world is made new, reordered from top to bottom. Of course, such remembering isn't just recollection of something absent, casting our minds back to the past, which has gone. It's remembering that is evoked and sustained by the fact that Jesus Christ, the one who there and then worked the world's salvation, is now present, ruling all things, through his Spirit bringing all things to their perfection. To remember him is to know not only where we've come from but where we are, who is with us: *Jesus, our peace.*

Second, therefore, we're called to know God. For Christians, knowing God means knowing God in Jesus Christ as the one in whom alone is our hope and world's hope. "Be still, and know that I am God. I will be exalted among the nations, I will be exalted in the earth!" (Ps 46:10). Such remembering and knowing, apparently so small, so insignificant, so hidden, are the ways in which the church tries to point out the truth of the world.

The truth is that the world is—despite everything—the place where God rules; the place where sin has been defeated; the place where we may act to make peace because peace has been made; the place where it's possible to resist evil because God has already resisted to the uttermost and overcome. To this God—the peace-maker, the healer, the reconciler, the judge, the ruler of all—be ascribed "glory, majesty, dominion, and authority, before all time and now and forever. Amen" (Jude 1:25).

PART II

SALVATION'S GOD

V I

WHO IS GOD?

AND one called to another and said:

"Holy, holy, holy is the LORD of hosts;
the whole earth is full of his glory!"

ISAIAH 6:3

The question which Trinity Sunday (first Sunday after Pentecost in the Western liturgical calendar) sets before us is very simple: Who is God? Who is the God in whose name we have gathered? Who is the God who is present with us? Who is the God who speaks to us of the salvation which he has accomplished for us in Jesus Christ? Who is the God whose power is unleashed among us like a living fire in the Spirit's work? The answer to the questions that Trinity Sunday offers to us is this: God is Father, Son, and Holy Spirit. This One is the God whom we've gathered to praise; this One is the one who has healed us from sin and made us new; this One is the one who renews our lives day by day and will bring us to perfect fellowship with himself. In other words, what the people of God celebrate today is the gospel's answer to the question: Who is God?

Now, when we start thinking about Trinity Sunday in those terms, things begin to look rather different. Most of us are used to the idea that the church's teaching about the Holy Trinity is baffling and have resigned ourselves to being baffled and leaving matters there—all that language about three being one, all that funny language about persons and relations and processions and all the rest. It seems light-years away from real, live Christian discipleship. But Trinity Sunday isn't about the *doctrine* of the Trinity; it isn't an opportunity for theologians to show off their talents in public. Trinity Sunday is not about a *doctrine*; it's about what the doctrine is *about*. It's about what the doctrine is pointing to—wonderful and life-giving truth.

What it indicates to us is this: that the God whom we confess in the Christian creed; the God into whom we're baptized; the God who is our savior and deliverer; the God in whom we trust and to whom we pray; the God to whom alone we turn in life and death is this one, the three-in-one, the thrice-holy one, the Father, the Son, and the Spirit. This is our God. This is God for us.

"Holy, holy, holy is the LORD of hosts" (Isa 6:3). It has long been a tradition in Christian thought and Christian worship to associate those words from Isaiah with the three persons of our confession of the Triune God. Where does that confession come from? If we are truly going to understand our confession of God the three-in-one, then we must start by saying something like this: the Christian confession of God as Father, Son, and Spirit isn't something the church made up; it isn't an arbitrary idea that somehow got stuck in the mind of the church. The church confessed God as Trinity for one reason alone: this is what God shows himself to be. This isn't what the church tells itself; it's what God tells the church about himself. God shows himself to be Father, Son, and Spirit in his revelation.

What is God's revelation? It's God's mighty arm bared for us; it's God's mighty hand outstretched to help us; it's God among us, showing himself to be our Creator, our Reconciler, our Redeemer. As God comes to us, he makes himself known to us. And he makes himself known to us as the Holy Trinity.

God makes himself known, first of all, as the *Father*. Who is God the Father? He is God who wills from all eternity to be God for us and God with us. In God the Father, we have God's unshakeable determination, God's eternal resolve, that he will not be God without us. God the Father chose us—from all eternity, from before the foundation of the world, before there was ever a creation or a creature, God the Father chose. That is, God the Father willed that there should be a creature living from his mercy and grace and delighting in him. God the Father chose us for fellowship with himself. He chose that he would be our God and we would be his people. And because he is this God, God is Creator of heaven and earth. He fulfills his purpose by making us for life with himself.

"In love he predestined us for adoption to himself as sons through Jesus Christ, according to the purpose of his will," Ephesians tells us (Eph 1:4–5). The decisive words are "in love." God the Father's eternal purpose isn't some terrible grim fate, some iron determination. It's the unshakeable character of his love. Nothing can deflect him from his loving purpose; no power can overwhelm him or turn him from what he wills. And what he wills as God the Father is to be with us as the heavenly Father of his children, as the one who is our Lord, protector, and deliverer. To believe in God the Father, then, is to believe that what the Christian gospel declares is really true: from all eternity, God is our God, our Father.

Second, this same God, the thrice-holy one of the Christian confession, makes himself known as God the *Son*. He destined us in love to be his children, the verse in Ephesians continues, "through Jesus Christ" (Eph 1:5). That puts the matter in a nutshell. In God the Son, the Father's will is put into effect. In God the Son, the Father's resolve is unleashed in the world. Above all, what the Son does is this: he reconciles sinners and so makes sure that fellowship with God is renewed.

In the Son, God faces the terrible reality of our sin. Why is sin so dark? Because at its heart, sin is a refusal to live in fellowship with God. It's a rejection of the eternal purpose of God the Father. Sin will not have life with God. It refuses to be a creature; it refuses to live from God, with God, and for God. Beneath all the different forms that human sin takes is a basic reality: *the sinner wants* to be rid of God, to be alone, self-reliant, self-making, undisturbed by God. That's why sin is destructive. It alienates us from God. Sin breaks that life-giving communion with God for which the Father makes us. But—and it is the most important "but" in the whole Christian gospel—God doesn't allow us to destroy ourselves by breaking free from him.

In the person of the Son, God comes to us and among us. He takes on flesh. In Jesus Christ, God the Son becomes man, and in doing this, he takes our place. He steps into our situation. He takes it all upon himself: our sin, our wicked rebellion, our stupid pride and self-reliance, our squalor, our awful separation from God. He takes it all upon himself, and as he takes it, he takes it away. He bears our sins; the whole weight of our sin falls on him, and he dies. But because the one who takes all this is God himself, because *he* is the sin bearer, our sins are cast away forever. He does what we can't ever hope to do for ourselves: he reconciles us to God. He reestablishes the peace and communion between God and his creatures. He makes lost sinners into God's children. He works the great miracle of reconciliation. That's why we confess that God is God the Son, our God, God for us.

As God the Father, God resolves to be our God. As God the Son, God ensures that his resolve will not be broken by sin but will triumph over our folly and wickedness. But there is more: the miracle does not stop in some bit of history two thousand years ago. The miracle of God's reconciliation extends toward us now: it's present and alive, at work among us. God himself is among us and in us, transforming our lives, renewing us. He renews us by setting us free from sin; he renews us by opening our ears to hear his word; he renews us by opening our mouths to speak his praise; he renews us by opening our hearts to know and love our neighbors. And he does all of this because he makes us share in the new life of Jesus Christ, the life of resurrection. How does God do all of this? He does it as the *Holy Spirit*. The Holy Spirit is God among us. The Holy Spirit is the one by whom all that God the Father wills and all that God the Son accomplishes becomes real and effective among us and in us. That is why we confess that God is God the Holy Spirit, the divine power who makes all things new.

It's this God whom the church confesses and praises as "holy, holy, holy is the LORD of hosts" (Isa 6:3). Why "holy"? Because this God, the one who encounters us, the one who makes himself known to us in his great works of salvation, is the majestic Lord of all things. He's God for us, unquestionably so. He isn't some domestic deity, some useful fiction to cheer up our lives. He's the one whose glory fills heaven and earth: utterly resplendent, utterly beyond, the one before whom we can only bow down. To encounter this one, as Isaiah encountered him, is to encounter one by whom we're absolutely dissolved: "Woe is me! For I am lost ... for my eyes have seen the King, the LORD of hosts!" (Isa 6:5).

And so for us: God is the *holy* Trinity, King, and Lord of all things. But that isn't all: for he is also, Isaiah says, the "LORD of hosts" (Isa 6:3, 5). Who is the Lord of hosts? He isn't our enemy. He isn't one who is simply an object of terror. He's the Lord of all the powers of heaven, the one whose limitless might is let loose— not *against* us but *for* us. "The LORD of hosts is with us," the psalm tells us (Ps 46:7). He isn't an absent God, locked up in his celestial court, closed off from us. He's the God who is enthroned in an *open* heaven; he's the God whose power is at work to support, save, and establish us. He's our "refuge and strength, a very present help in trouble" (Ps 46:1).

Such, then, is the one whom we confess and praise on Trinity Sunday. We confess and praise God the Father, who wills from all eternity that we should be with him. We confess and praise God the Son, who loves us and comes to us in mercy, bearing our sins and reconciling us to God. We confess and praise God the Holy Spirit, who gives us life in fellowship with God. We confess that this one, the Holy Trinity, is the Lord of hosts, who is with us. That is the Christian answer to the question, "Who is God?"

What difference does this make? It makes all the difference in the world, for one very simple reason: this God is real. He is among us now; he has gathered us to himself in fellowship; he speaks to us in his word; he beckons to us from his table to come to him to be forgiven and reassured; he offers himself to us, that we may love him and have faith and hope in him. That's why in the old prayer book collection for Trinity Sunday, we're told that our faith in God the Holy Trinity is a "defense against all adversities."

I don't know what particular adversities you may be facing, together or on your own. If you're an average congregation, there will be adversities enough: worries about health, jobs, children, marriages, and loneliness; guilt and anxiety about whether God will accept us; shame about the past; fear about the future, and all the rest. God's word says this to us all as we face whatever adversity has crossed our paths. You may trust this God. His will is for your good, and it can't be shaken. He has proved that to you in his Son, and he is now with you in his Spirit.

And so, to this God—Father, Son, and Holy Spirit, who lives and reigns for us from eternity to eternity—be ascribed all might, majesty, dominion, and power, now and forever. Amen.

VII

GOD FOR US

FOR the grace of God has appeared, bringing salvation for all people, training us to renounce ungodliness and worldly passions, and to live self-controlled, upright, and godly lives in the present age, waiting for our blessed hope, the appearing of the glory of our great God and Savior Jesus Christ, who gave himself for us to redeem us from all lawlessness and to purify for himself a people for his own possession who are zealous for good works.

TITUS 2:11–14

One of the basic rules for understanding the Christian gospel is this: grace and godliness must never be separated. The truth of God's mercy and the reality of God's call to purity are indissolubly bound up together, for the gospel isn't only about God's gracious intervention to rescue us from sin—it's also about God's command. It concerns the new life of obedience and holiness that must follow from our rescue. The gospel isn't only about good works, about living under the command of God; it's also about the astounding gift that God gives us, a gift that we don't deserve and can never earn.

Gift and call, promise and command, mercy and obligation: always and everywhere, the gospel keeps them together. It keeps them together as two great realities that surround the individual life of the Christian believer and the common life of the church of Jesus Christ. On the one side is the miracle of God's mercy to the unholy and the unrighteous; on the other side, the no less real and no less powerful reality of God's summons to holiness and righteousness. So here, in the letter of Titus, this priceless fragment of Christian exhortation, God's grace has appeared with a twofold purpose: to redeem and to train, to save and to purify. "The grace of God has appeared" (Titus 2:11).

What is grace? Grace is God's active mercy. It's a mercy that is utterly unexpected and unhoped for. Grace is that great initiative—wholly without desert, with no cause other than sheer goodness—in which God looks upon the ruin of the human situation and acts to heal, repair, and renew. Now, this grace, the apostle tells us here, has *appeared*. It isn't an idea or an abstraction. It's neither dream nor hope. It's a reality given to us, set before us in human form and action; it's a *life*. God's grace is visible, embodied mercy, and it's visible and embodied in one place: Jesus Christ. He literally *is* grace; his coming to us, his words and deeds, his passion and death, and his indestructible resurrection life: all *that* is what is meant by grace. He is our great God and Savior Jesus Christ, and so he is grace manifest, grace active among us.

The question that the apostle is here addressing is this: What impact does this visible grace have on the way we live? What does this gospel of the appearance of grace mean for the life and activity of those for whom it is visible? Accosted by this grace in its inescapably real form in Jesus Christ, what kind of people are we commanded to be? To all this, the apostle gives two answers.

The first thing he says is this: the heart of our moral lives is not what we do but what Christ has done. The Christian gospel means renouncing worldly passions and living upright and godly lives, but those things are always a consequence of what God in Jesus Christ has done. Godliness *follows* grace. The core of living a life of purity before God is summed up in what the apostle says about Jesus Christ: he "gave himself for us" (Titus 2:14). He—his sheer generosity, his unsparing giving of himself to sinners—is the grace which makes it possible for us to live in obedience to God. That giving of himself can be described as two things: it is *salvation*, and it is *redemption*.

The grace of God has appeared for the *salvation* of all. He gave himself for us in order to save: to rescue us from the lostness and suffering and condemnation, which we have pulled down upon ourselves. He gave himself for us, entering our accursed situation, taking it upon himself and so taking us out of the absolute peril in which we had landed ourselves. As the one who *saves* us, he is also the one who *redeems* us from all iniquity. He buys us out of slavery to evil; though we're hopelessly bound to the wicked tyranny of sin, robbed of our freedom, and living in fear and darkness, he pays for our release; he takes up our cause; he sets us at liberty. He is Savior and Redeemer, God *for us*.

The apostle is telling us: this is where we stand. This is the truth about our lives. Because of the appearing of this unimaginable grace of God in Jesus Christ, we're the saved and the redeemed. And that means that by that grace our lives have been entirely recast; our situation has been entirely remade. In our lostness, he has given us a place and a direction. In our alienation he has restored us to life and fellowship with God. In our pollution he has cleansed us. In our condemnation he has made us righteous. He has made us new.

However, it's at just this point that we often begin to get stuck. "How can this be true?" we ask ourselves. "How can it really be true that my life has been transformed by God's grace, that it really is made new? It looks just like the old life; it's the same me—the same habits, the same failures, the same evasions." Anyone who struggles seriously with the Christian life very soon has to face real disappointment; for all that salvation has come to me, for all that I have been redeemed from iniquity, iniquity seems still to have a pretty firm grip on my life. And if that's true—if I'm still a determined sinner in spite of everything that God has done for me—then do all these great claims about salvation and redemption mean nothing at all in the end?

What are we to say to this? We often give ourselves a false answer to those questions. It's false because, though it seems to solve the problem, it actually makes things far worse. The false answer is this: if the reality of salvation is to be real in me, then it has to be done not just *for* me but *by* me. I've got to make it real. And I've got to make it real by moral effort. God provides the impulse; I perform the moral work. God makes it possible; I make it real. It's an attractive answer; it beguiles us more than anything because it presses us to take responsibility for our moral living. But it's false, and it's destructive.

It's false, because it says that God doesn't really save us and redeem us but that we do that for ourselves. It's destructive, because it places an unbearable burden on us, the burden to perform to prove ourselves before the judgment seat of God. When that happens—when we tell ourselves that we make the gospel real by good works—then what we've done is changed a gospel truth into a moral demand. Grace has become not just command but also threat. Countless Christian lives have been bruised by this, made wretched and unhappy by the terrible conviction that we have somehow to certify our salvation by good works.

The muddle and misery that this lands us in comes from a basic mistake. The mistake is thinking that the new life of a Christian is only real when I make it real by living the new life of obedience. If we're to set aside the mistake, we need, instead, to say something like this: it's precisely *because* salvation is already real that I venture the life of obedience to God. Obeying God's call, heeding God's commands, struggling to live a righteous and godly life: I do all this not to make my salvation secure but because it is already secure, over and above anything I am called to do.

Because God in Jesus Christ really is our Savior, because he is really *for us*, because the grace of God has appeared and transformed our situation from the ground up—then I live the Christian life not to prove to myself and everyone else that the gospel is true, but because the gospel is already the most true and real thing that there is. The rule is not "live a holy life in order to become holy."

Rather, the rule is: *live a holy life because you have already been made holy*. Live the life of righteousness, because you are righteous; act as one of the saints of God, because that is who you are.

Can you see the freedom in all this? It's freedom from condemnation, from that self-imposed condemnation that makes miseries of us all; freedom from being my own savior and redeemer. That kind of freedom in the Christian life and the peace that kind of freedom brings—they are the fruit of realizing that grace really is grace, not half-grace; that God's mercy goes all the way, not just part of the way; that the appearance of that grace in Jesus Christ really is effective, really is all-powerful, really does what it sets out to do, which is to make the world a new place.

All that being the case, the apostle says a second very important thing here: *grace trains us for active godliness*. Talking about God's grace doesn't mean that we can sit back and forget living a life of godliness and righteousness. It doesn't mean the end of the Christian life of holiness.

It's a real mistake to think that good works are proof of our salvation, but it's just as real a mistake to think that good works are a mere irrelevance. The point of the gospel isn't that the way in which we live our lives doesn't matter—it does matter, but not for the reason we usually think. Holiness and the life of obedience matter because they're the most natural and truthful way of living in the light of God's grace. In Jesus Christ, salvation and redemption have appeared, and that appearance sheds its light on everything because it's the new truth of the whole of human life.

If we're to live and act truthfully, we must live and act in accordance with what God, in Christ, has done. For the grace of God has a purpose; salvation and redemption are not just an empty declaration but are full of power to transform and redirect our lives. Grace is for us, and because it's for us, it turns our lives around and sets them off in a new direction of obedience to God.

It's for this reason the apostle talks of God's grace in Jesus Christ not only as a gift but also as something which *trains* and *purifies* (Titus 2:12, 14). Grace, he says, is "training us to renounce ungodliness and worldly passions, and to live self-controlled, upright, and godly lives in the present age" (Titus 2:12). Grace is instruction. It's only instruction because, first of all, it is mercy. But it's a mercy that instructs us, because it says to us, in effect, "You must live in the new world which God in Christ has established." Because of the appearance of salvation, unfaithfulness to God and worldly passion and ungodliness have been ruled out of court; they have no place in the new world in which Jesus Christ reigns; they are *untruthful*.

Therefore, if we want to live truthfully, we must follow the gospel's instruction. That means letting it train us to act well: to set aside all the things that God has once and for all set aside in Jesus Christ and to work at all the things which he declares to be the way to live in fellowship with himself. In practical terms, this means that we're to set aside *irreligion*.

Irreligion means false conceptions of God, those lies in which we substitute a fantasy about the divine for the revealed truth of God's grace. But it also means the practical secularity in which we refuse to be bound to God: the neglect of God in which we make our way through much of our daily business as if God doesn't matter (or at least doesn't matter very much). Again, we're to resist worldly passion, for when God is no longer revered, then all our other desires get tangled up, and we're torn apart and robbed of stability. God's grace, therefore, trains us to act in a self-controlled, upright, and godly way: self-controlled in keeping our inordinate desires from breaking loose; upright in living in fellowship with our neighbors; godly in yielding consistently to the good purposes of God. This isn't works-righteousness; it's simply living out of the way Jesus Christ has made the world to be.

Moreover, this grace which trains us also *purifies* us. The purpose of the redemption of God in Christ, the apostle tells us, is "to purify for himself a people for his own possession who are zealous for good works" (Titus 2:14). Grace has a goal, and the goal is a people. Two things are to be said of that people. They're a people who are possessed by God—that is, who stand in a distinctive relation to God, sanctified by him, set apart for him, determined by him for fellowship with himself. And because they're his people, they're people who are lit up with a particular passion. That passion is a zeal for good works.

To sum up: What kind of place is the world? It's the place in which God's grace has appeared; it's a world full of God's generosity. It isn't lost and unredeemed; it's the place where salvation and redemption are real and manifest, in which God is for us.

How then should we live? We must trust ourselves wholly to that grace, confident that it has done for us what we cannot do: it has made human life new. We must let that grace train us, let it shape our lives so that we act in ways that are fitting and truthful.

I don't know what struggles you face in your individual life and in your life in gospel community. But if you partake in an average Christian community, then there will be at least two sorts of folks there. There will be those relaxed Christians who are tempted to think that the gospel lets them off the hook, that God's forgiveness means that we needn't struggle to be pure because God has already made us part of the family. To them, the gospel says that God's mercy is at the very same time his command; grace is a call as well as a gift. There will be others, the worriers, who are tempted to feel that the gospel is just another set of crushing demands—that it requires purity, and purity is utterly beyond us. To them, the gospel says that grace is a gift before it is a call.

And to both the relaxed and worriers, the gospel says: "The grace of God has appeared, bringing salvation for all people, training us to renounce ungodliness and worldly passions, and to live self-controlled, upright, and godly lives in the present age, waiting for our blessed hope, the appearing of the glory of our great God and Savior Jesus Christ, who gave himself for us to redeem us from all lawlessness and to purify for himself a people for his own possession who are zealous for good works" (Titus 2:11–14).

May God give us grace to trust the gospel and to adorn it by our actions, to his glory and our comfort. Amen.

VIII

GOD WITH US

THIS is my commandment, that you love one another as I have loved you. Greater love has no one than this, that someone lay down his life for his friends. You are my friends if you do what I command you. No longer do I call you servants, for the servant does not know what his master is doing; but I have called you friends, for all that I have heard from my Father I have made known to you. You did not choose me, but I chose you and appointed you that you should go and bear fruit and that your fruit should abide, so that whatever you ask the Father in my name, he may give it to you. These things I command you, so that you will love one another.

JOHN 15:12–17

At the heart of the life of Christian discipleship is the mystery of divine election. To be a follower of Jesus Christ, to be in the circle of those who gather around him and live in union with him, is to be determined and appointed by God. It's to exist by virtue of the divine decision. The content of that divine decision is that God sets apart a company of men and women for fellowship with himself. It's a decision by God that there should be a people of God: established by him, bound to him, called together for his glory and for their own glorification. Election means fellowship; it's God's unshakeable determination to be God with us, and his equally unshakeable purpose that we should be with him.

To be with us is the theme of all God's works and ways with his creatures, beginning with the creation of humankind, continuing in God's calling of the patriarchs, and in his gathering of the people of Israel to himself. It finds its culmination and its center in the ministry of the Son of God. In the Lord Jesus, there takes place the very core of God's election; in him, God's calling of humanity into fellowship is reestablished and completed. Around him, there gathers the company of the people of God. At first it's a ragtag set of characters, the little band of disciples who scatter at his death; then, as he is raised to new life and enters into his glory as ruler of all things, and as he sends the Spirit to summon humankind to fellowship with him, then there is the great company, the holy church throughout all the world—including, by some miracle, us. And of that company—and therefore of us, too—the Lord Jesus says this: "You did not choose me, but I chose you" (John 15:16). What does this mean?

It means, first, that there is a negative aspect to the reality of God's election. Election is an absence of human willing. Fellowship with God is not a matter for human choice; we do not direct ourselves to this. We do not create fellowship. It comes to us as a divine decision. As a *decision*, note—not as an offer that we're required to accept before it's real, not as a possibility set before us, which we must turn into something actual, but as that which has been established about us and for us, independent of our choosing. In this matter we aren't consulted any more than God consults his creatures before he creates them. Nothing precedes God's choosing—no human goodness, no human aspiration, no desert or need or worthiness: nothing but the sheer freedom of God. It's that freedom, directed toward us, that is the second, positive aspect of election: "I chose you" (John 15:16). So then, election is the triumph of God's will to fellowship. Over against the absence of human self-determination is the decision of God in which he determines to be God with his people.

Crucially, this determination is *mercy*. It's not mere fate. God's choosing isn't just a matter of his assigning some to this category, some to another. It isn't random or arbitrary or graceless. It's an act of love, of limitless love, in which God creates and sustains us so that we can know and enjoy him and find our well-being in life with him. It isn't the act of a despot who pushes the world around on a whim and who cares nothing for his subjects; it's the act of God the Son, who lays down his life for his friends.

We will understand very little of the Christian gospel unless we understand this: election is a way of talking about God's pity for us, of saying that God chooses us not merely in order to exercise his will but in order to help us, that God's election of us is the only thing that stands between us and our self-destruction. God's election is his utter determination that we will flourish, his steadfast and tender mercy that holds us fast. It's the authority with which he takes from us our evil capacity to undo ourselves and sets us under the conclusion of his love.

It's for this reason, therefore, that election extends God's consolation to us. It's consolation above all because it's election to *friendship with Christ*: "No longer do I call you servants ... but I have called you friends" (John 15:15). Election has a purpose, and that purpose is friendship with the Lord Jesus, a friendship that is the essence of what it means to be a Christian disciple.

What is involved in that friendship? In part, friendship with Christ is a matter of being befriended by one who gives everything for us, who seeks our well-being even at the cost of his own life, which he lays down for us. He befriends us. On no other ground than that of his love, he draws near to us, taking upon himself the ruin and squalor that we have made of our lives, ending the terrible isolation from God in which our sins have landed us, loving us by grasping us and separating us from our sins. And yet there is more: in making us into his friends, the Son of God also shares with us the secrets of heavenly wisdom given to him by the Father. "The servant does not know what his master is doing; but I have called you friends, for all that I have heard from my Father I have made known to you" (John 15:15).

To be befriended by Jesus, then, is not just to be dragged along behind him without a clue as to what is happening, just swept up in his wake. It's truly to be with him, and to be given *knowledge*. To be his friend is to live in the truth which he reveals to his friends. His friendship once and for all dispels the ignorance and darkness of human life apart from God. It isn't blind fellowship, but a fellowship which brings the gift of insight and wisdom and knowledge of God. Jesus befriends us, and as he does so he teaches us, helping to see and know and live from the truth.

All this, then, means that, very far from being a kind of bleak divine decree, God's election is about the way in which he restores communion between us and himself. In the face of our weakness and misery and pride, God ensures that what he purposes for us stands fast; and what he purposes is that he should be our God, and that we should be his people, knowing the one who knows us and loving the one who loves us. And that purpose is fulfilled in the calling together of God's people by the Son of God: "You did not choose me, but I chose you" (John 15:16).

There is, however, one more matter here. Election is not only determination and mercy. It's also appointment. To be elect is to be determined by God to act: "I chose you and appointed you that you should go and bear fruit" (John 15:16). Election is not only God, as it were, giving us a status; it's also God giving us a certain task. What is that task? Here it is described as *bearing fruit*. The fruit is, very simply, the fruit of love of God and love of one another. "This is my commandment," says Jesus, "that you love one another as I have loved you" (John 15:12), Or again: "These things I command you, so that you will love one another" (John 15:17).

Love is the renewal of human fellowship. Love is seeing my neighbor as someone given to me, someone who stands before me as what they are, and who faces me with an obligation. If I am to love my neighbor, then I may not turn from them; I may not dismiss them as too ignorant or foolish or demanding or different. I must recognize in them a summons to fellowship and service, a call to lay aside what I think of as my good and, very simply, to help my neighbor; I must make my neighbor's cause my own. More than anything, I must come to see that my neighbor presents me with a command. The command is, of course, not simply that of my neighbor, but the command of Jesus himself. It's his, Jesus', commandment to which my neighbor's need gives voice. It may be a pretty squalid or demanding or thoroughly inconvenient voice; nevertheless, in it we hear him: "This is my commandment" (John 15:12).

Now, this task of responding to my neighbor's summons as the summons of Jesus isn't one in which we're left to our own capacities. God doesn't appoint us to a task which we must undertake unaided. We bear fruit only insofar as we live in union with Jesus Christ, the branches drawing their life from the vine (John 15:5). "Whoever abides in me and I in him," Jesus says earlier in John 15, "he it is that bears much fruit, for apart from me you can do nothing" (John 15:5). And that is precisely what it means to say that we're chosen by Jesus: we aren't apart from him; we aren't struggling along trying to make our lives half-decent, always threatened by failure and guilt. We are *his*, bound to him, not by bonds of our own tying, but by bonds which he himself has tied and which cannot be dissolved. We're his friends. Chosen by him, subject to the miracle of his grace, we're destined to live with him. And chosen by him, we're appointed by him to acts of human friendship.

The world is a sad and frightening place; its greatest sadness is its ignorance of the gospel in which alone it can find healing and reconciliation. But God has set an end to that ignorance. He has done so in the person of his Son, and in the little company which has been chosen to be with him. We are that company; to us it has been given to know the truth of Jesus Christ and to hear his commandment. May God give us grace both to hear and to obey, for our own sake and for the world's healing. Amen.

IX

GOD AMONG US

AND this is the testimony of John, when the Jews sent priests and Levites from Jerusalem to ask him, "Who are you?" He confessed, and did not deny, but confessed, "I am not the Christ." And they asked him, "What then? Are you Elijah?" He said, "I am not." "Are you the Prophet?" And he answered, "No." So they said to him, "Who are you? We need to give an answer to those who sent us. What do you say about yourself?" He said, "I am the voice of one crying out in the wilderness, 'Make straight the way of the Lord,' as the prophet Isaiah said."

(Now they had been sent from the Pharisees.) They asked him, "Then why are you baptizing, if you are neither the Christ, nor Elijah, nor the Prophet?" John answered them, "I baptize with water, but among you stands one you do not know, even he who comes after me, the strap of whose sandal I am not worthy to untie." These things took place in Bethany across the Jordan, where John was baptizing.

JOHN 1:19–28

For any alert reader, one of the most striking features of the gospel stories is the *questioning* that is evoked by the coming of Jesus. Jesus and the events surrounding him precipitate the most urgent and intense questioning, because the coming of Jesus means conflict and upheaval. His coming disturbs, and as it disturbs, it not only bewilders but it provokes opposition. The advent of God's Messiah tears the world open; it sets before those who are privy to it something that astonishes and affronts, and so it generates questions—irritated questions, questions that are the expression of deep frustration and offense, questions that seek to challenge and suppress the uncontainable reality of the advent of Christ. Above all, the question so often thrown at Jesus is: "By what authority?"

Now, those whose lives are caught up by this upheaval—those like John the Baptist—are also caught up in the questioning. Here, in our text, John is faced with the stark demand to give account of himself: "Who are you?" (John 1:19). Yet, as we shall see, what is most striking about his answer is its indirectness. He answers the question of who he is by speaking not of *who he is* but of *what he does*: he is the voice of the herald who speaks; he is the one who baptizes for repentance. In just this way, in this very elusiveness, he demonstrates the secret of who he is—he is in himself nothing; he is simply the God-given witness to the coming of God's Messiah.

First, then, the question: "Who are you?" (John 1:19). The question comes from the priests and Levites—roughly speaking, the temple clergy and the police—who have been sent from the center, from Jerusalem, to investigate John and his ministry. The question isn't particularly friendly or particularly curious. But it's an anxious question, because John is clearly turning heads and causing a stir. In a charged and volatile religious culture, full of exciting expectations about the coming of the Messiah, who knows what is going on? Maybe, who knows, this wild man on the edge of the city is part of the beginning of the end. And so, on behalf of their chiefs, the priests and Levites ask, really wanting to know: "Who are you?"

John's answer is, of course, singularly disappointing. He apparently deflects the question, and instead of declaring his identity, he tells them not who he is but who he is *not*. "I am not the Christ," he says. "'What then? Are you Elijah?' He said, 'I am not.' 'Are you the Prophet?' And he answered, 'No' " (John 1:20–21). Why does he do this? Why is he so apparently evasive, so hard to pin down?

Part of the answer may be that John the writer of the Gospel wants to steer his readers away from any veneration of the Baptist—the very strong words of the Baptist's denial that he is the Christ could suggest this: "He confessed, and did not deny, but confessed, 'I am not the Christ' " (John 1:20). But there is a deeper point here, which is decisive to understanding the meaning of the story of John the Baptist, and it's this: in and of himself, John is nothing. John's denial—his repeated "I am *not*"—is crucial to understanding who he *is*. As he answers that intrusive demand, "Who are you?", he must first say what he is not, lest he be thought of as having some dignity or status or consequence in and of himself. For the mystery of John is precisely his strange emptiness, the absence of any prestige or rank in him. That's why he turns his questioners away from himself. They have been sent to get an answer; they want John to line himself up with a category or a title like "prophet" or "Messiah," and they want to use that to place him and explain him. They want to be able to put a name to the disturbance that they find in him and so set some limits to it. They want to make him the kind of religious event that they can handle. But John refuses to be lined up, and he refuses because if he were to give in to the request, he would be fundamentally false to his true calling. He would make himself an object of interest, a figure with some independent standing, and thereby he would cease to be who he is.

And so, "I am not the Christ" (John 1:20)—for it's the essence of John that he points away from himself and to the other, to the coming one who alone is God's anointed. Nor is he Elijah (John 1:21)—that is, he is not Elijah returned in fulfillment of the prophecy of Malachi that before the great and terrible day of the Lord the prophet Elijah would appear once more. Nor is he the shadowy figure of "the Prophet" (John 1:21)—a figure raised up by God at the end times to declare the consolation of Israel. He's not these things because if he were, then he would be something, and that something would, as it were, get in the way—it would hinder him in being what he truly is.

The old prophets could, of course, claim an office and distinction. Standing between God and God's people, speaking the word of the Lord, they acted as mediators between the Lord of the covenant and his people, and in the prophet's voice could be heard the voice of God. But not so John the Baptist. He's not called to the office and work of mediator. He simply is called to be utterly transparent to the one who is to come. He is a mere appendix. Of himself, he's of no interest; what matters is only that to which he points. He doesn't seek a hearing for himself; listening to him is merely preparatory to listening to this other one, the coming one, the great teacher who will speak with the voice of God himself. "John," says Augustine, "gives place"—and that puts the matter in a nutshell.

What this means is that the real answer to the question of who John *is* is given by trying to grasp what he *does*. He is in himself of no importance, a mere sign indicating another. What matters, therefore, is his work of indicating the coming of God's Messiah. And that work of indication is twofold: he speaks, and he baptizes.

He indicates the coming of God's Messiah by *speaking*. "They said to him, 'Who are you? We need to give an answer to those who sent us. What do you say about yourself?' He said, 'I am the voice of one crying out in the wilderness, "Make straight the way of the Lord," as the prophet Isaiah said' " (John 1:22–23).

John is a speaker. He lifts up his voice, but he doesn't do so to say anything about himself or to bear testimony to his own cause. Quite the opposite: he lifts up his voice to speak of another, to bear witness to another's cause. It's the sheer anonymity of John that is so striking here. In the same way that John forswears the office and dignity of prophet in order that Christ alone be magnified, so here: he is simply "a voice." What matters isn't the speaker but what is said. Augustine, again, says this: it is as if John were saying, "I am prophecy itself." The clue to John, the deep secret of his mission and ministry, is: "After me comes a man who ranks before me, because he was before me" (John 1:30).

John indicates the coming of God's Messiah by speaking, and he speaks thus, the gospel tells us, "in the wilderness" (John 1:23). He does not speak from the seat of prestige in Jerusalem, not in the temple or even in the synagogue, but outside. In the wilderness of the sour history of the elect people of God; in the sheer waste and perversity of Israel's hostility to God and God's mercy; in the barrenness of Israel's attempts to arrest the course of God's grace and channel it into itself and preside over it—in all this desolation, John speaks. He does the one thing that above all things must be done: he speaks of the coming of God's Messiah. As he does so, he beckons and stretches toward the miracle that is about to step onto the scene.

He testifies that God's dealings with God's people are not at an end. God has not withdrawn himself; God has not been excluded; even the sins of God's people, even their wicked attempts to possess God, have not driven God from them. On the contrary: God himself is on the way, directing his paths toward his people with inexorable judgment and even more inexorable mercy. And because this is true, then John also testifies to what more than anything else is required of God's people. Because the Lord of the covenant is coming to his people, because this is the time of his advent, then they must "make straight the way of the Lord" (John 1:23); they must clear away every obstacle and make in the desert a highway for God. And, above all, John testifies to the sheer presence of God's Messiah. "The next day," the Gospel continues, "he saw Jesus coming toward him, and said, 'Behold, the Lamb of God, who takes away the sin of the world! This is he" (John 1:29–30).

So John indicates the coming of God's Messiah by the action of his speaking. Second, he indicates the coming of God's Messiah by the action of his baptizing. It was, we can probably assume, John's baptizing that attracted the attention not just of the crowds but of the officers of society. And his baptizing attracted that sort of press because it seemed to be the sign of the fact that John had some sort of special significance, some noteworthy role as an agent in the saving work of God. Having failed to get a straightforward answer to their question, "Who are you?," the priests and Levites get a bit edgy about John's evasiveness and worry that they might have to go back to their masters empty-handed. So they press him: "Then why are you baptizing, if you are neither the Christ, nor Elijah, nor the Prophet?" (John 1:25). But John's reply makes things no better at all for his interrogators. For he tells them that his action of baptizing is like his word of testimony: it's not about him, but about another.

As with his speech, so with his baptism: it indicates. It indicates the cleansing that is required in the face of the coming of the Lamb of God. He—the Lamb of God, not John—is the one who cleanses from all sin; his baptism, not John's, will be the baptism with the fire of the Spirit, which destroys unholiness and sanctifies the people of God. There's no power in John's baptism, no force or capacity of its own. The content of his baptism is simply this: "Among you stands one you do not know, even he who comes after me" (John 1:26–27). John's baptism is testimony, a pointing to the coming Messiah who will baptize with the Holy Spirit and with fire.

What does this curious material have to say to Christian people as we stumble through the wilderness of life? The first thing to say is this: no less than its original hearers, we stand beneath this witness. John lifts up his voice and addresses *us*. We aren't superior to it; we aren't free to consider it from afar as some curio from the past, some fragment of a long-gone religious culture to which we cannot conceivably belong. What we encounter here is testimony, a testimony that we aren't at liberty to ignore. The burden of that testimony is this: "Among you stands one you do not know" (John 1:26).

There is a whole spiritual world in those few words from the Baptist. What we might hear in them is something like this: God's

Messiah, Jesus the Christ of God, is *present*. He is among us, and because he is present, God himself is present.

However crazy it may seem, we somehow have to grasp that in the gatherings of the gospel community is the presence of the Lamb of God, who takes away the sin of the world. The purpose of our assembly is to be confronted by testimony to the gospel. The burden of that testimony, at its most basic and its most pointed, is that our lives stand under one all-encompassing fact: the fact that among us stands Christ himself.

But—and this is the point at which that testimony confronts us and confounds us—the presence of Christ goes largely unrecognized. It's not known. It's refused, or confuted, or held at a distance, or ignored: anything but acknowledged. "He was in the world," John told us earlier in the Gospel, "yet the world did not know him" (John 1:10). It's just that dynamic that is repeated in all times and all places, including our own. It's the struggle between God's self-giving, merciful presence and the ignorance that refuses to know.

If, therefore, there is a point to our gatherings, it has to be this: We must turn from our ignorance. We must cease in our efforts to wish away the presence of Christ. We must confess what above all we fear to confess—that he stands among us. In this way we must make straight the way of the Lord. How do we do this today? By listening repentantly to the voice of the herald, John the Baptist, letting God unleash this witness upon us, declaring to us its judgment and so enclosing us in its compassion and grace. Augustine once more: "Christ lighted for himself a lamp by which he might be seen, and that lamp was John." Amen.

X

GOD ABOVE US

In saying, "He ascended," what does it mean but that he
had also descended into the lower regions, the earth? He
who descended is the one who also ascended far above all
the heavens, that he might fill all things.

Ephesians 4:9–10

For most of us, I suspect, the ascension of Jesus is a rather
peripheral bit of Christian teaching. We often can't see the
real force of believing in the ascension. At first sight it seems to
tell us nothing that's not already told to us by the resurrection—
namely, that Jesus is exalted to share in the life of God, to be Lord
of all things. Rather easily, the ascension comes to be not much
more than an extra ornament, a flourish at the end of the story
of salvation that we can safely bypass without missing anything
of real importance. If we do let the significance of the ascension
sink into our minds and spirits, however, we come to see that it's
a crucial episode in the mystery of salvation.

Here, in the exaltation of Jesus at his ascension, we reach a
culminating moment in the drama of God's rescuing the world
from peril. Here we face that point in which the movement of the
incarnation, the passionate descent of the Son to take upon himself the fate of the world, is completed by his triumphant return
to the side of the Father. Here, at his ascension, he has declared
to us just what has taken place in the death and resurrection of

the Son: his work is finished; his salvation is realized; his rule is established as universally real and effective. Here we have the completion of the great sequence—from exaltation to exaltation through the depths of separation; from heaven to heaven, the great royal progress of God through abasement to victory.

He who ascended, Ephesians tells us, is he who descended (Eph 4:9–10). Both his descent and his return to glory are accompanied by a sign. *The sign of his descent*—his taking flesh—is the sign of the virginal conception and birth of Jesus. That sign tells us that God's coming in the flesh is wholly a divine initiative; his coming in Jesus is a pure gift of pure grace; the initiative is God's alone. And so also the glorification of the Son at the end of his saving work is accompanied by a sign: *the sign of the ascension*. His work finished, the Son now enters again the divine majesty that is his, taking up his rule at the right hand of the Father. If the virgin birth shows the sovereignty of grace in the absence of human initiative, the ascension shows that same sovereignty in the majestic act of the enthronement of the Son.

He has ascended, Ephesians tells us, "far above all the heavens" (Eph 4:10). What does this mean? One thing it doesn't mean is that Jesus is now remote, unavailable, having finished his work and withdrawn from us. It means, rather, that as the ascended one, Jesus is present, but present in the way that God is present.

In the New Testament's accounts of Jesus' existence after his death, there's a curious mix of absence and presence: he both is and isn't with his disciples. He is, to be sure, visible, knowable: he speaks, he eats, he commands, he consoles, and he promises to be with them. And yet the way in which he's with them seems to include his absence, his withdrawal. When Jesus ascends, Luke tells us at the beginning of the Acts of the Apostles, the same Jesus who promises to be with his disciples until the end of the ages is "lifted up, and a cloud took him out of their sight" (Acts 1:9). He simply disappears. Yet this doesn't mean that the ascended Jesus is simply a figure on the fringes of our lives, not one to be reckoned with. His distance, withdrawal, and otherness are not negatives.

Rather, they alert us to something that is quite crucial to understanding Jesus' presence as the risen and ascended one, which is this: Jesus is present in the way that God is present. We have Jesus as we have God. Jesus' presence with us isn't natural but spiritual.

To say this is not to say that he is not *really* present—we have to be very clear about this point. The spiritual character of his presence doesn't mean that his presence is something *less* real. Affirming that his presence is a spiritual reality has nothing to do with the idea that it's some kind of psychological mood; "spiritual" doesn't mean less than objective. What is spiritual is not ethereal; it's that which has the reality of God, and therefore that which is ultimately real, real in absolute abundance, gloriously and dazzlingly real. But spiritual reality is not like natural or created reality. It's different, above all, because spiritual reality is present as it gives itself. It's not inert, just there before us like houses and trees and buses. It's not just another bit of the world. Spiritual reality *makes* itself present, gives itself to us. It's present in grace, lovingly bestowing itself but never at our command. So with the spiritual presence of God in the risen and ascended Christ: it is pure gift. The ascended Christ can't be forced to appear as we can force a person to appear before a tribunal or command the presence of a servant. The risen and ascended Christ is present in his own way, in his own time, at his own good pleasure, because he's present in the majestic freedom of the Lord God himself.

From this we can perhaps begin to see the grand logic of the Christian confession, which we make when we recite the Apostles' Creed. That simple affirmation of faith condenses the whole scope of God's great work of salvation to one integral movement, the movement of the Son of God from eternity to eternity. Conceived by the Holy Spirit, he comes in the miracle of God's condescension. Born of the Virgin Mary, he takes on our flesh. Suffering, crucified, buried, he is obliterated by our separation from God; in our place he descends into the depths, into the hell that we have made. Then the great act of exaltation: he rises again, since death cannot not hold him; he ascends to heaven; he sits at the

right hand of the Father, his work complete, his triumph acknowledged, his glory manifest.

But why does all this matter? Why is this any more than just
a set of abstract ideas? The answer is simply this: the whole
movement of the Son of God, his descent to the depths and his
ascent far above the heavens, is for *us*. This movement, this great
sequence of God's works, is the true history of humankind. Here,
in this man's birth and death, resurrection and exaltation, a final
judgment about human life is made. Whatever else we say about
ourselves, this above all must be said: this history involves us.
Here, we're remade.

This, in the end, is what baptism is about.[1] To baptize a child
isn't to give a child a religious start in life, still less is it a naming
ceremony. It's saying something about what God has done and
is doing and will do for this child. And what it says is this: this
child's life is caught up in the saving death and resurrection of
Jesus Christ. God grasps this child's life; God declares that this
life is governed by the single fact that Jesus Christ has died, is
alive, and rules all things.

The ascended Jesus is for us, and for us in three ways. He is for
us as prophet; he is for us as priest; he is for us as king.

The ascended Jesus, first of all, is *prophet*. He himself manifests
himself; he himself makes himself known in the world.

We're often perplexed by the question of how Jesus can be
real to us: How can this figure from so far away, so long ago, be
a real factor in human life? Is he not light-years from us, histori-
cally, culturally, religiously so distant as to be unattainable? If we
fret about those issues, we may be led to try and fill up the gap,
to bridge the distance between us and him with all sorts of things.
Maybe, we might think, it's something the church does that makes
him real: its worship or its service in the world, we may want to
say, makes him present, delivers him into our midst. Or maybe it's
something that individual Christians do: maybe he's real because

---

1. Note to reader: this message was delivered on the day a baptism was performed.

we make him real through vivid religious experiences. But whatever way we try to make Jesus Christ real, the whole process is simply pointless. He doesn't need to be made real to us, because he *is* real to us; he doesn't need us to help him along a bit, give him a hand to gain a hearing. He declares himself; he manifests himself; he makes himself known in the world. And he does so as the ascended one who is *prophet*.

Jesus Christ the ascended one *speaks*. He is not mute; he does not lack a voice with which to make himself known. He is prophet, outgoing and communicative, declaring the truth about himself. How does he do this? He does it through his word and his Spirit. That is, he declares himself through the the word of the apostles, which we call holy Scripture, and he declares himself through the Holy Spirit, in which his word is impressed on our hearts with truthfulness and authority as the word of the true prophet. The ascended one is not, therefore, some distant Lord of whom we know nothing and hear even less; he is himself the living Word of God whose voice fills the creation.

Second: the ascended Jesus is *priest*. In the Christian tradition, the ascension of Jesus is linked to his intercession on our behalf before the Father. He appears before the Father as our advocate and intercessor. And his priestly work is not fragile, vulnerable, a hesitant attempt to persuade God to forgive. It's utterly authoritative, utterly effective, utterly reliable, because it's the intercession of the Son of God himself, whose saving work is finished; whose sacrifice for us has been offered and accepted; and who is now empowered to act as the advocate for sinners.

All of that means that we are *forgiven*. The terrible domination of the past, the whole muddle of what I have so far made of my life, does not enslave me because I am forgiven, and that forgiveness is sealed, made effective and real to us, by the ascension of Jesus.

There are, I believe, quite staggering lessons here for the life of faith. Christian people are very often deeply afraid of their own failures. Older Christians are, I suppose, especially vulnerable because they've had to face and struggle with wickedness, their own and other people's, and have come to see that it can wreck human life. But faced with this dark knowledge, many of us make a mistake. We may turn in upon ourselves to try and find the resources to deal with our own propensity for evil: "If only," we say, "I had more discipline, more moral and spiritual energy, I wouldn't be defeated by evil so much of the time." In particular, we may begin to turn to conscience as the true guide, the reliable voice that will keep us on the straight and narrow. Yet it never quite works.

Conscience is a good servant but a fearsome tyrant of a master. Give conscience the job of pronouncing absolution, and you will soon find yourself the victim of a merciless enemy. Conscience does not forgive; conscience accuses. Conscience doesn't free us from our sins; it binds us to them. It ties us tighter and tighter to our wrongdoing by setting it always before us: "This is who you are! This is what you have done!" And it's that voice of the accuser which is finally silenced by Jesus himself, the ascended priest. He alone—not conscience—is authorized to secure our forgiveness. He alone is empowered by the Father to pronounce to us absolution, to break the bondage of the past, and to set us free.

Third: the ascended Jesus is *king*, Lord of all things for the church of God. He sits at the Father's right hand—his work finished and accepted, he occupies that place of majesty and undisputed rule which is God's alone. He is subject to nothing, to no one; but all things are subject to him. He is above: effortlessly superior to rules and authorities and names, superior for all times and in all places; everything is under his feet. All this, Ephesians tells us, is *for the church* (Eph 1:22). The majesty and glory in which he governs all things are purposive and directed, and what they purpose, what they're directed toward, is the community of the people of Jesus Christ.

Jesus Christ, the exalted one who is king, prophet, and priest, is the sovereign Lord turning to us in mercy and grace. In him heaven is open to us—that is, human existence has a future beyond death, in fellowship with God in Christ. Indeed, in one very real sense for the New Testament we're already exalted with him, seated with him in the heavenly places, liberated from the kingdom of death and even now possessing the heaven that he has secured for us. In him hell has been set aside.

Hell is everywhere: in sickness, in worry, in loss of hope, in loneliness and guilt. But, Ephesians tells us, when Jesus Christ ascended on high he led a host of captives—that is, he demonstrated that all that is opposed to him and his will for human life has been stripped of its power. We know our own hearts and their terrors, but more than that, we know also that over against them stands the single fact of him, risen, ascended, glorified, and bestowing life on his people through his Spirit.

And that is why we pray:

Grant, we beseech thee, almighty God, that like as we do believe thy only-begotten Son our Lord Jesus Christ to have ascended into the heavens; so we may also in heart and mind thither ascend, and with him continually dwell, who liveth and reigneth with thee and the Holy Ghost, world without end. Amen.

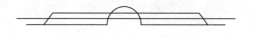

PART III

SALVATION'S HEART

XI

THE FAITHFUL WITNESS

GRACE to you and peace from him who is and who was and who is to come, and from the seven spirits who are before his throne, and from Jesus Christ the faithful witness, the firstborn of the dead, and the ruler of kings on earth.

REVELATION 1:4B–5A

What does it mean, first of all, to confess that Jesus Christ is the "faithful witness" (Rev 1:5)? Let's begin here. There is in human life, as a whole and in each of us individually, a very deep desire to evade the truth. Such is the disarray of our lives that we find truth very hard to bear. We find it hard to bear because when we talk about truth, we're talking about something that will not, in the end, yield to our wills.

The truth about the world is something over against us, something that we cannot subdue. Truth cannot be commanded; instead, it commands us—it forces us to acknowledge that the world and we within the world are what they are, independent of us. Truth blocks invention; when we reach the truth, we reach the limits of our wills. And it's because truth is that kind of barrier against us that we have to find ways of circumventing it. We have to flee from the truth. Sometimes we do that by simply hiding from it, "living a lie," as we say. More often, we turn all of our skills to the task of modifying, reinventing, and massaging the truth so that it's no longer quite so threatening and may become rather more friendly to what we want. We may do this by adding to the truth or by subtracting from it, but the result is the same: that fatal fall into illusion that is one of the bleak bits of human corruption.

It has become a commonplace that a lot of late modern culture is built on just such modifications of reality: in politics, the media, and elsewhere, image is all, and substance counts for very little. But such things are merely the contemporary manifestation of a deeper decay. That deeper decay is the one great lie that afflicts us all: the lie that God does not see us and that we are safely out of reach of his truth. "Woe unto them that seek deep to hide their counsel from the LORD," says Isaiah, "and their works are in the dark, and they say, Who seeth us? and who knoweth us?" (Isa 29:15 kjv). It's a fearfully destructive lie—above all, because it cuts us off from the reality of God and unleashes on us all manner of misery and distress.

Now, it's this situation that God takes upon himself in the life and mission of Jesus Christ. In and as this one, Jesus, God enters into this hopelessly spoiled state of human illusion and does for us the one thing which we cannot do to ourselves: he attests the truth. He refrains from doing what we all do: he does not conspire with falsehood. And he does what none of us do: he lives by and declares the truth. It's for that reason—because he does not lie, but testifies to the truth—that he is confessed as the "faithful witness."

As *witness*, Jesus Christ is, literally, martyr: his life and existence, his word and work are a pointing to, an indication of, the truth. He is simply and completely his testimony to what is really the case. He makes no compromises and undertakes no evasions. He does say what is not, and he does not fail to say what is. He is, as John's Gospel puts it, "full of … truth" (John 1:14). And his witness is *faithful*—that is, his witness is persistent, unhesitating, reliable, and permanent. His truthfulness is utterly durable; it doesn't break down under the temptation to make a truce with lies or half-truth. It simply says what is, and acts in accordance with what is, and so rejects.

No one can read through the Gospels without realizing the quite terrifying effect of his witness upon those who are encountered by it, for his witness illuminates. In his speaking and showing of the truth, those who encounter him find themselves confronted by one who unmasks them, who shows them up for what they are. Above all, encountering him means being shown up as those who have fled from the truth and preferred falsehood; who shun the light and choose darkness; who are caught in the ghastly trap of untruth in which they are both deceivers and those who are deceived. Such truthful witness is, of course, of a quite different order from mere psychological acuteness.

His witness to the truth is not that of the therapist or friend or counselor who slowly leads us out of our illusions to face ourselves and the world without the protective armor of our illusions. His witness is of a wholly different order: it's the divine manifestation of truth; it's judgment and revelation. By it, those who encounter this one are absolutely disturbed, summoned, not just to a more orderly and integrated dealing with reality but into an entire reordering of their world. They must dismantle a whole way of lying their way through life—or, more accurately, they must somehow come to see that the entire edifice has already been brought crashing to the ground by the truth speaking of the Son of God.

There is a climactic moment in the passion story of John's Gospel where Jesus testifies before Pilate: "For this purpose I was born and for this purpose I have come into the world—to bear witness to the truth. Everyone who is of the truth listens to my voice" (John 18:37). And Pilate said to him: "What is truth?" What are we to make of Pilate's reply as he turns away from Jesus to return to his accusers? Skepticism? Perplexity? The weary cynicism of the hard-pressed man of affairs? All of these—but above all, evasion, an attempt to slip away from the terrible directness of Jesus' testimony, somehow to hide from that fact that unlike all others, Jesus hasn't made his peace with falsehood but has confronted it at every turn. "I have come into the world—to bear witness to the truth" (John 18:37). For Pilate and the rest of us, that witness is such that by it our lies and evasions are destroyed.

But those lies and illusions aren't destroyed before the faithful witness is himself annihilated. The faithful witness, Revelation tells us, is also the "the firstborn of the dead" (Rev 1:5). "Fear not," the glorified Christ announces, "I am the first and the last, and the living one. I died, and behold I am alive forevermore, and I have the keys of Death and Hades" (Rev 1:17–18). "*I died*," he says. Why did he die? Because his faithful witness was unendurable; because the purity with which he testified could not be borne, and so by oppression and judgment he had to be taken away.

His death was the culminating episode in the conflict which marked the whole of his existence: a conflict between prophecy and falsehood, between witnessing to the truth and quenching the truth at all costs. But—and this is nothing less than the key to who he is—his death is not the triumph of the kingdom of falsehood, but its overthrow. He isn't simply a martyr who speaks the truth to its opponents and dies for the privilege. His death isn't one more casualty in an untruthful world. No! In his death a whole world of pretense and deceit is eliminated.

How is it eliminated? It's eliminated by his resurrection, because he is alive; because he is "the living one," risen from the dead (Rev 1:18). And his resurrection from the dead demonstrates that the final weapon of the kingdom of falsehood has been broken. That final weapon is the pretended power of falsehood to silence the truth by putting its witnesses to death. But Jesus Christ, the first and the last and the living one, cannot be silenced by death. He shares in the undefeated lordship and truthfulness of God; he is "who is and who was and who is to come" (Rev 1:8), and his witness cannot be extinguished. The truth that he announces and for which he dies is unbreakable. "Behold I am alive forevermore, and I have the keys of Death and Hades" (Rev 1:18). In him, truth *reigns*.

And that is why the faithful witness, the firstborn of the dead, is "the ruler of kings on earth" (Rev 1:5). He is truth; and because he is truth, he is life; and because he is both truth and life, he is power. In the end, falsehood does nothing; it is powerless to generate life, and it can only diminish and destroy it. But truth is potent, and the power of the faithful witness is supremely legitimate and righteous, for it maintains truth and quickens us to life. Negatively, this means that by the rule of this truth, our autonomy is finally chastened.

It's the habit of the kings of the world to think that their power is unrestricted, that there's no point at which they reach a limit. This is a habit of the great men and women of power, of the magnates of business and sport and entertainment, and even of little lords in the miniature kingdom of academia. But we're not rulers, any of us—we're ruled; we're subjects.

But, positively, giving up our self-government and consenting to the truth of Jesus' faithful witness is to our great and endless comfort. It brings, as John tells us, "grace and truth" (John 1:14). It's the truth of our reconciliation, our healing, our restoration to fellowship with God. It's the truth which clears away all the idols which we have used to bolster up our lives. It's a truth that does not deal out death but rather gives the gift of life with God. It's a truth that sets us under the protection and care of the one Lord who alone seeks our well-being and will not abandon us to falsehood.

What, then, must we do? We must attend to the faithful witness of Jesus Christ. We must hear and receive his testimony. We must subject ourselves to its scrutiny, its exposure of our folly and fabrications. We must let it put to death our untruth and give us the gift of life. We must consent to its rule over us, knowing that it is the generous and good rule of our Maker and Redeemer. But we can only do these things if God helps us in our distress and incapacity.

And so we pray:

We beseech thee, O God, the God of truth, that what we know not thou wilt teach us, and from that is false and hurtful thou wilt evermore defend us; through Jesus Christ our Lord.

Amen.

XII

THE GREAT REVERSAL

HE has delivered us from the domain of darkness and transferred us to the kingdom of his beloved Son.

COLOSSIANS 1:13

The feast of Christ the King on the Western liturgical calendar is the celebration of our deliverance. It's the joyful confession and acknowledgment of the great reversal that has taken place in human life. For over this feast of the church there stands the quite extraordinary truth that human life—our lives—have been caught up in God's great work of separating us from the misery of sin and setting us in the kingdom of Christ. In this celebration we confess and exult in the fact that Christ is king, and to confess and exult in that kingship is to know that our lives are rooted in and built on this reality above all: in him we really do have redemption and forgiveness.

He rules, and because he rules, the world is full of redemption, full of forgiveness. The world is his kingdom; it's a world in which redemption and forgiveness are not just hopes or ideals or values but realities, secured by his lordship and shared with the world through his Spirit.

This great work of deliverance, we may note, is as it were inserted between a negative and a positive. The negative is the dominion of darkness. The positive is the kingdom of God's Son. And in between those two states lies a single dramatic and decisive work of God in and as Jesus Christ. We look first at each of these, the negative and the positive, and then move to ponder a little the redeeming act of God that effects our deliverance from darkness into the Son's kingdom.

First: "He has delivered us from the domain of darkness" (Col 1:13). What is this dominion of darkness? What may we say of it?

Simply and comprehensively, the dominion of darkness is the tyrannous reality of life apart from God and opposed to God. To be human apart from God is to live under the most destructive tyranny imaginable. Sin means bondage; sin makes us into the helpless subjects of a very ruthless and hostile dictator. Of course, we don't realize this—that's part of the tyranny. We think we're free; we think we're lords of all. We think that we've finally broken our bonds and finally achieved the mastery for which we've been longing. We *think* we've emerged from the benighted state of being subject to God into the light of determining our own lives. We think that, but in fact we're in bondage and in darkness.

The kingdom we put ourselves in as sinners is not a realm of freedom and the full light of day—it's a gloomy kingdom; it's only half-alive; it's not a place of freedom but of wretched subjection to an alien and ruthless force. And the force is after us with a vengeance—it does not seek our good, but our hurt; it wants to destroy. We break free from our moorings, but when we do that, when we break our tethers to God, then we're simply at the mercy of the vile and monstrous regime of darkness.

That regime is *lawless*. That means that it's a kingdom with no truthful order to it. It's not a rule founded upon the good order of God. It's not a kingdom that bases itself on the will of God for human life. It doesn't follow God's purpose. It's a lawless kingdom, a kingdom that has broken free of the form in which human life flourishes. And so it's a nightmare place, a place with no shape. We've seen often enough in recent history what happens to human political society when law breaks down: life becomes unlivable because there is no continuity, no roles, no duties and rights, and above all, no structure. And because it's lawless in this way, it's also *illegitimate.* It's based on nothing but sheer pretense, the pretense that it is a valid kingdom, that it is a proper way of living human life when in fact it's nothing of the sort. It's an utter sham. It has no calling from God; it has no power from God; it has no part in the purposes of God. It's wholly and irredeemably false.

Because of all of this, it's an accursed kingdom. Life within the order and purpose of God is life that is blessed. That is, life under God's rule is life precisely set in the way of flourishing, because it is in relation to God the life-giver, the God whose ways bless us by tying us to himself. But detached from God and God's ruler, we aren't blessed, but cursed. We draw down upon ourselves all the malignant and life-destroying consequences of cutting ourselves off from the Source of our life. More than anything, we suffer. This stupid and malevolent kingdom in which we put ourselves does nothing to our good and everything to our hurt. It makes us victims and slaves.

The kingdom of darkness is indeed a fearful place: tyrannous, lawless, and accursed. But for all that, we haven't said the most important thing that is to be said. The most crucial thing to be said about this kingdom isn't the fact that it's dark and destructive but something quite contrary. The most crucial thing to be said about the kingdom of darkness is that it has been overthrown. It's a reality which has been abolished and destroyed. It has met its master, finally and definitively, in Jesus Christ. Its tyranny has been cast down; an end has been put to its lawlessness; its curse has been taken away. If it continues to exist, it isn't as some grand competitor to God, some monstrous power that God must take seriously and which threatens even now to overwhelm God and God's people. It continues only as a shadow, only as that absurdity to which God in Christ has said, "No!"

How can we say that? How can we say that the tyrannous realm of darkness has been cast down? In saying such things, don't we invite the reproach that we are just fantasizing, and worse than fantasizing—aren't we just sweeping away the appalling history of human sin and suffering as if it didn't matter? That charge would be entirely just if we were simply, as it were, projecting some picture that all is well, dreaming up some ideal world in which the kingdom of darkness has no place. But we're not dreaming when we say that the dominion of darkness has been cast aside. We are simply repeating the sober truth of the gospel. And the sober truth of the gospel in this matter is this: he has "transferred us to the kingdom of his beloved Son" (Col 1:13).

What abolishes the dominion of darkness is not fantasy, or desire, or a cry of need; no, what abolishes that dominion is the sheer abundant reality of God's kingdom in Jesus Christ. We do not live under the tyranny of darkness, and we do not do so because between us and that darkness God sets the single absolute fact of his Son. He, Jesus, his name, is reality, is the kingdom and rule of God. He is the overthrow of darkness; he is and he secures the inextinguishable light of God's salvation. In him and as him God establishes the kingdom of salvation.

"He has … transferred us," Colossians says (1:13). *He* has transferred us. If we've been lifted out of tyranny, it's because of him, God in Jesus Christ. If there's a kingdom of salvation, it isn't by virtue of anything we've done or been. Our will and action is utterly beside the point simply because we're entirely without capacity. We can no more transfer ourselves into God's kingdom than we can fly, and so our rescue is his affair alone. *He* has transferred us. And he *has* transferred us. Christ's deliverance of us from darkness isn't some distant event yet to be realized, some hope that we may stretch toward but which we can't count on here and now. He has already done this; it is finished business; at his cross and in his resurrection he has already achieved fully and perfectly and sufficiently our transferral out of darkness into his kingdom of light. It's a past accomplishment and therefore a present reality and promise.

This reality in which we now stand—the kingdom of his beloved Son—isn't vacillating, or unsure, or fragile. It's a reality that has the force and effect and eternity of God himself. Into that reality he has *transferred* us. We have been lifted out of one realm and placed securely in another. He hasn't, note, called us to transfer ourselves. He hasn't invited us to cooperate in the work of transferral. He hasn't empowered others to do it on his behalf. He has directly and sovereignly snatched us up and set us down again and thereby decisively altered our situation. Once for all—by the mystery of his incarnation, death, and resurrection, and by his glorification to reign with God in all eternity—he has accomplished the great work of deliverance. And—astonishingly—this is true not of other people or of some mythical human race. It's true of us: it's us whom he has transferred. We're no longer left languishing in the gloomy world of sin; we're no longer in the dominion of darkness; we're in the kingdom of his beloved Son.

What are we to say of this kingdom into which we've been transferred? Most simply and clearly, it's the kingdom of the Son of God. In this kingdom he reigns; here he is supremely alive with sovereign and undefeated power. It isn't the pretended kingdom of darkness; it isn't a place of misery and undoing. It's that realm in which there rules God the Son, the one through whom and for whom and in whom all things were created (Col 1:16). It's the kingdom of Jesus Christ—he isn't some minor dictator, some petty tyrant out to take us for a ride; he's the one who is before all things, and the one in whom all things hold together (Col 1:17). There's no other ruler alongside him; he rules over the entirety of human life and history alone, because in him "all the fullness of God was pleased to dwell" (Col 1:19). And because it's his kingdom, it's a kingdom of light, not darkness.

Those who are in that kingdom are the "saints in light" because the light of Jesus Christ, the power with which he rules this kingdom, is "glorious" (Col 1:11–12). It's utterly radiant; it blazes with the light of God; it banishes and excludes darkness. And, again, as it's the kingdom of light, it's also and equally the kingdom of redemption, of forgiveness, and of reconciliation.

And, finally, therefore, this kingdom is supremely legitimate and lawful. It's the place of order; it's the sphere in which human beings can flourish because it's a place where they fulfill the will of God, where they can live according to their natures under the governance of the good hand of God. And all this—the glory of this orderly kingdom of peace and reconciliation—is rooted in the fact that the kingdom bears his name, the name of Jesus, the one in whom the Father wills that the creation should be saved.

To say these things is to do nothing more than scratch the surface of this astounding reality, to do nothing more than make a gesture toward something so compelling that it begs description. The kingdom of darkness is finished; the kingdom of Jesus Christ is the supreme reality. What, we may ask by way of closing, are we to do in the place where we've been established by God? What does this reality require of us?

It asks, first, that we acknowledge it; that we confess its sheer and abundant reality; that gladly and unaffectedly we confess that what we read of here is true and wholesome and good. It asks us to give our joyful consent to the fact that this is how things really stand with us. There's a lifetime of learning and unlearning involved here. To see these things—to see that this kingdom really is how things stand—isn't a momentary impulse but the fruit of long and disciplined and loving attention to the gospel. It involves a setting of the will, a refusal to be deflected into letting the kingdom of darkness have its say, a determination not to be negotiated, threatened, or bullied out of the gospel. It involves, in short, faith—that casting of ourselves on the righteousness, truth, and goodness of God.

But it also asks that we ourselves live in the world in a different way. There aren't two kingdoms in the world, the kingdom of darkness and the kingdom of light. There's one kingdom, which is the kingdom of Christ. There aren't two gods, but one God, the God and Father of our Lord Jesus Christ. And it's the task of the church of Jesus Christ and of each member of the church to rise up against the great lie that there are two kingdoms; to strive energetically and courageously against the idea that Jesus Christ isn't really Lord of all things. To confess that Jesus Christ is the one who is before all things is to say this: no person, no power, no institution, no form of human life, no sorrow and disaster, can overthrow his rule. And because that's true—because Jesus Christ is King—then we may rise up against the whole regime of pretense, and we may calmly and cheerfully and courageously say: in everything he is preeminent.

> Almighty and everlasting God, who hast willed to restore all things in thy well-beloved Son, the King and Lord of all; mercifully grant that all peoples and nations, divided and wounded by sin, may be brought under the gentle yoke of his most loving rule; who with thee and the Holy Spirit liveth and reigneth, ever one God, world without end. Amen.

XIII

SHAPED BY LOVE

THE next day again John was standing with two of his disciples, and he looked at Jesus as he walked by and said, "Behold, the Lamb of God!" The two disciples heard him say this, and they followed Jesus. Jesus turned and saw them following and said to them, "What are you seeking?" And they said to him, "Rabbi" (which means Teacher), "where are you staying?" He said to them, "Come and you will see." So they came and saw where he was staying, and they stayed with him that day, for it was about the tenth hour. One of the two who heard John speak and followed Jesus was Andrew, Simon Peter's brother. He first found his own brother Simon and said to him, "We have found the Messiah" (which means Christ). He brought him to Jesus. Jesus looked at him and said, "So you are Simon the son of John? You shall be called Cephas" (which means Peter).

The next day Jesus decided to go to Galilee. He found Philip and said to him, "Follow me." Now Philip was from Bethsaida, the city of Andrew and Peter. Philip found Nathanael and said to him, "We have found him of whom Moses in the Law and also the prophets wrote, Jesus of Nazareth, the son of Joseph." Nathanael said to him, "Can anything good come out of Nazareth?" Philip said to him, "Come and see." Jesus saw Nathanael coming toward him and said of him, "Behold, an Israelite indeed, in whom there is no deceit!" Nathanael said to him, "How do you know me?" Jesus answered him, "Before Philip called you, when you were under the fig tree, I saw you." Nathanael answered him, "Rabbi, you are the Son of God! You are the King of Israel!" Jesus answered him, "Because I said to you, 'I saw you under the fig tree,' do you believe? You will see greater things than these." And he said to him, "Truly, truly, I say to you, you will see heaven opened, and the angels of God ascending and descending on the Son of Man."

JOHN 1:35–51

We can't go too far in reading the Gospel accounts of Jesus without grasping that his presence and activity constitute a fundamental disturbance of human life and calling. The arrival of Jesus, his eruption onto the scene, means interception: human life and history stop dead in their tracks. What intercepts human life in this way is the new call that Jesus issues to fellowship with God and service in God's kingdom.

His call is a *new* call. He isn't simply stirring up fresh devotion to a call issued long ago; he isn't simply urging a return to faithfulness, to a vocation that he knows his hearers have already received and which they only need to reactivate. Much more is Jesus reconstituting the people of God, starting the covenant afresh. Henceforth, because of his call, the people of God will be *God's* people because they are *his* people, those who hear *his* summons. Because of the presence and activity of this one, Jesus, a new determination is made concerning human life. Placed in his presence, hearing his word, humanity is summoned to new life in his company.

The story of the calling of the disciples is one of the key points at which the Gospels set before us this recasting of the whole human situation. Those stories, in their varied versions, present the disciples as examples of the radical recasting of human life that Jesus generates.

The calling of the Twelve is a sign, an initial and very powerful instance, of what's to be true of humanity as a whole. In their calling, in their being bowled over and remade by the sheer fact of being drawn into Jesus' company, we're to discern what's true of all who find themselves face to face with God's Son. Like them, we're to see ourselves as gathered around him. Like them, we're chosen to live in fellowship with him, having the fundamental impulse of our lives in his presence and calling.

As we probe the Gospel stories a bit more, however, we find that the various writers present two rather different sorts of accounts of this calling to discipleship. The first sort of account is that in Matthew, Mark, and Luke. Although each of those Gospels has its particular emphases, they share a common presentation of the calling of the disciples. All of them present the story as a vivid, crisis-filled encounter in which Jesus issues a command to discipleship, the one called dropping everything to follow him.

The command of Jesus, as Matthew, Mark, and Luke present things, isn't a gentle invitation or even a strongly-worded suggestion. It's imperious! It expects no opposition; it invites no reflection or pondering of issues but requires immediate, life-changing, absolute obedience.

The vividness of their presentation derives from its extraordinary simplicity. More than anything else, what they want to get across to us is the unopposed effectiveness of Jesus' call. His simple command, "Follow me," places the hearer in an entirely new situation: *hearing that summons*. All that the disciple can do is follow—henceforth they *must* attach themselves to him, they *must* be in his company and at his service.

What Matthew, Mark, and Luke have for us, if you want, is the nearer, more proximate description of the call of Jesus, in all its immediacy and shock and disorientation. But John gives us something rather different. What he has to say is certainly not incompatible with what's happening in the other evangelists, but it has a different feel to it, a difference in tone and presentation that alerts us to a rather different purpose. If the other Gospel writers give us a proximate depiction, John gives us an ultimate account of what is going on. He tries to pierce to the heart of the matter. And the heart of the matter, according to John, isn't simply the drama of encounter between the prophet Jesus and an assortment of bewildered fishermen and others. The heart of matter is the eternal purpose of God.

It's the particular genius of John's portrayal of Jesus to set the events of the gospel story in an ultimate context. To read his Gospel is to be taught with a directness and depth found nowhere else in the New Testament that the history of Jesus is the very presence before us of the purposes of God. John seeks to school us into the conviction that is surely the marrow of Christian belief: that these events in the gospel story, these people in these encounters, are caught up in nothing short of the laying bare of the absolute. Above all, it's John's particular task to try and press into our minds and souls the fact that in this one, Jesus, we're placed before the very being of God, God's Word and self made flesh for us. And so as John leads us through the events of Jesus, he's charting for us how all that takes place has to be seen as the breaking into time of the final, eternal reality of God.

It's this, I think, which comes to expression here in John's rather mysterious presentation of the calling of some of the disciples. What's most of all important for us to listen for in our reading of the passage is that there is a different center of gravity in John's account of the matter. In the other Gospels, the distinctive note is Jesus' direct, imperious, critical summons: Follow me. But in John, things are different. The actual calling by Jesus, the spoken summons, is by no means the heart of the story. Rather, what happens in John is the disciples simply gather themselves around him, as if drawn by invisible threads. In a mysterious, almost dreamlike way, the little group assembles around Jesus, like the chorus of a play collecting itself around the central character. Quietly, unresistingly, the company who will live in fellowship with Jesus comes together.

And it does so, not because he has to take some initiative and pull them all into his presence, but simply because this is the way it's to be. There's an atmosphere of inevitability over the whole episode. What happens seems to be taking place as it has been determined to happen long ago. And Jesus himself is effortlessly in command of the whole scene. He does almost nothing and says very little apart from responding to questions. He certainly is not a herald, crying aloud to try and set something in motion. It's as if he has known these people from all eternity and has been waiting for them to arrive in their allotted places at their allotted time, there to fulfill the purpose of God.

So, we take notice of what he says to Nathanael: "Before Philip called you ... I saw you" (John 1:48). From all eternity Nathanael is seen and known by Jesus. Before all of Nathanael's acts and words, before all his questions and troubled hesitations about this strange person before whom Philip has brought him, there's the seeing and knowing of the Son of God. And what is true of Nathanael is true of all the others who gather in his presence. They find themselves face to face with one who is before them, who introduces them into a reality which from the very beginning has been his purpose for them.

To put it simply: John is saying that discipleship is God's decision, not theirs. They are what they are because of the eternal will of God. As John's story sets out their calling, we're given the sense of the supreme objectivity of the will of God for the lives of these people. There's something unquestionable and *given* about the new reality that God brings about in Jesus Christ. What happens when they stumble into the presence of Jesus is nothing other than the disclosure and confirmation to them of God's purpose.

This, we might say, is what *is*; this is how things are. And so when these people come face to face with Jesus, it's not as if they're called to some heroic act of self-dedication. They aren't required to prove their worth or to strive to make themselves fit for this calling of God. No vivid demonstration of willingness is required. They're simply made aware of something that has *already* taken place: they *have been* chosen, they *have been* elected to know this one who already knows them. What's required of them is simply consent: that loving, free recognition of the decision of God as the only truth about them.

That's why the response that the disciples make is not some great oath of allegiance, some statement of their steadfastness and determination. They don't say anything about themselves at all. They talk of him. Faced with the completeness and irreversibility and unquestionable reality of the divine decision, they simply acclaim Jesus, the one in whom that decision seeks them out and establishes itself. They give voice, not to their own dedication to him but to the word and work of God, which is already complete, in which they find themselves transposed. Faced with him, they glorify God in his Son: "We have found the Messiah! ... You are the Son of God! You are the King of Israel!" (John 1:41, 49).

Such, then, is John's story of the calling of the disciples of Jesus: the mystery of God's eternal election set out before us in the lives of these particular men. What might this rather strange and distant story have to say to us? What may we take from what we read for our own instruction? Two things seem to me of especial importance here.

First, *we're also Christian people because of the decision of God.* We're Christian believers, members of Christ's people, because we share in something in which these men in our story also shared: God's gracious setting apart of a people for himself.

Like Nathanael and Simon and Andrew and all the rest, we're what we are because of a determination that God has made about us—that we will be his people; that we will be extracted from the hands of sin and death and given the gifts of righteousness and life; that we will live in the fellowship of God's Son. These things are true of us, because God wills that they should be. To realize this is to come to see that there is an infinite depth to the Christian life. The life of faith, the life of the disciple of Jesus Christ, isn't a mere human undertaking, some fragile, wavering commitment of ours, some decision we make but might well unmake if things should go differently. The miracle of Christian faith and discipleship lies within the hands of God.

We're what we are because of who God is, what God does, how God decides for us. "He chose us in [Christ]," the letter to the Ephesians tells us, "before the foundation of the world, that we should be holy and blameless before him. In love he predestined us" (Eph 1:4). Severed from that, Christian faith and commitment are just a perilous undertaking on our part, a shot in the dark. Why do we say it's more than that? Ultimately, because we know that we're known, that a decision has been made about us, that in Jesus Christ our destiny is not only offered but secured for us.

Second, *to realize the truth of these things is to be taught to praise God.* "You are the Son of God," says Nathanael (John 1:49), astonished by the fact that he is known and summoned by God in Christ (John 1:48). And so for us: to know God's determination of us is to be set free for praise. A deep sense of the decision which God has made about us does not lead us to be sullen or passive or fretful about the encroachments on our precious freedom. It leads to amazed acclamation of the most radiant and wholesome and deep reality: the reality of Jesus Christ himself.

This in itself ought to dispel the atmosphere of doom and gloom that often seems to hang around the ideas of election and God's determination of our lives. We have rather quickly decided that all this is just so much bleak fatalism, some dreadful iron necessity forced on us by a God of flint. But if what John is telling us has anything to it, the opposite is the case. To know God's election is to know that we're shaped by love, that we're called into being by mercy, that we're sustained by infinite goodness. And it's to know that such love and mercy and goodness are true to the very core of God's being.

If we're to know this properly, however, we must set our hearts on it. We must love what God commands. As always in the Christian life, the real issue is learning to desire what God really is, ordering our hearts to the truth of God. One of the forgotten worthies in the history of Christ Church is the seventeenth-century Puritan theologian and chancellor of the University of Oxford,

John Owen—the most considerable Oxford Christian thinker of his day, now all but eradicated from our corporate memory because he ended up on the wrong side of the debate in the restoration of the English monarchy (circa 1660). Besides being a theologian of real substance, Owen was also a spiritual writer, a man whose soul was utterly gripped by the reality of God.

He wrote a great deal on what he called the "spiritual affections," by which he meant that the Christian life is indeed one long struggle to love what God loves, to fix our minds and souls and desires on the truth and beauty that is God. He wrote this: "Spiritual affections, whereby the soul adheres unto spiritual things, taking in such a savor and relish of them as wherein it finds rest and satisfaction, is the peculiar spring and substance of our being spiritually minded."[1]

If we want to live our Christian lives well, if we want to be spiritual people, we need to love the right things, to learn to delight in what is truly delightful. And one of the things we need to learn to set our affections on is the destiny that God has had for us from the foundation of the world. We need to set our hearts on the fact that we're called into the company of his Son. When our affections are so engaged, then our minds will be set free to know and our mouths set free to praise.

---

1. *The Grace and Duty of Being Spiritually Minded*, chap. XI.

XIV

OPEN TO JUDGMENT

AND to the angel of the church in Sardis write: "The words of him who has the seven spirits of God and the seven stars.

"I know your works. You have the reputation of being alive, but you are dead. Wake up, and strengthen what remains and is about to die, for I have not found your works complete in the sight of my God. Remember, then, what you received and heard. Keep it, and repent. If you will not wake up, I will come like a thief, and you will not know at what hour I will come against you. Yet you have still a few names in Sardis, people who have not soiled their garments, and they will walk with me in white, for they are worthy. The one who conquers will be clothed thus in white garments, and I will never blot his name out of the book of life. I will confess his name before my Father and before his angels. He who has an ear, let him hear what the Spirit says to the churches."

REVELATION 3:1–6

One of the basic functions of the Bible in the church is to act as a critical corrective. That is, it's one of the primary jobs of Scripture to make sure that the life of the church is open to judgment. Scripture isn't only a sort of repository of received wisdom, or a source of consolation, or a story of the ways and works of God. It's all these things, of course: it counsels, consoles, and tells stories. But it also *judges*. It has a strangely intrusive task: sometimes quietly, sometimes spectacularly, but always with divine force and truthfulness, it sets our lives in the light of the truth. That's why reading the Bible isn't a tame business: these texts that we read day by day when we meet to worship in community aren't the domestic chit-chat of Christianity. They're part of the great struggle of which we and all Christian congregations are part—namely, the struggle between God and sin, between truth and untruth.

Of course, Scripture doesn't judge on its own authority or with its own voice. Scripture announces God's judgment. Scripture is the point at which our untruth is exposed, because it's the medium through which God communicates. Scripture bears witness to the fact that God isn't distant, inert, and mute but eloquent: God is the God who sees and speaks the truth.

Therefore, one of the things that it means to be a Christian community is to be those who are faced steadily by this intrusive word, to be a community that assembles around this text, because—however painful and disturbing and dismaying it may seem—hearing what it has to say is the way in which we are healed: healed from loss of truth, healed from that silence about unrighteousness and sin that is so profoundly destructive of human fellowship and flourishing. Being a community of the word of God doesn't mean having some industrial-strength *theory* about the inspiration of the Bible, and it certainly doesn't mean being a church that is satisfied with just brandishing biblical slogans as if they were weapons. It means something that is both more unsettling and in the end more fruitful: very simply, it means being a community that is ready to hear what the Spirit says to the churches.

We start here because the letters to the seven churches early on in the book of Revelation are almost impossible to understand unless we grasp that something like this is going on. In each of these passages, John the seer is instructed by the risen Christ to write a letter to what's called the angel of seven different churches, which is probably a way of saying that he is to address the words to the presiding spirit of each community. But, crucially, the words he is to write are not his own: they're *given*, and given by the Lord Jesus himself.

These messages are to be seen as far more than just a bit of encouragement or chivvying along. These are apostolic messages: they're a speaking called for by Christ, a word from God because of the Word of God. They're the "words of him who has the seven spirits of God and the seven stars" (Rev 3:1). The point of such language is to stress the utter dignity and unqualified authority of the one who here speaks through John's mouth. What's to be said isn't some partial, human judgment; it's not some opinion that can be weighed and perhaps accepted or perhaps repudiated; it's not a private view, one more thing to consider. It's the speech of Christ. These words are the words of the one from whose mouth, we have learned, there issues the sharp two-edged sword, the one at whose feet the church is to fall as though dead. It's he who speaks. What does he say?

He says, "I know your works" (Rev 3:1). He is, very simply, the one who sees and declares the truth. And his seeing and declaring the truth cuts through all human illusions, all human evasions. It's part of the perversity of our sinful natures that we operate with the crazy idea that God doesn't see what we're doing. We think we're safe; that God doesn't know, God doesn't see, that we can live out our lives hidden away, invisible to God, and immune from judgment. This is, indeed, a crazy idea, a kind of madness, yet very deep within the human heart is a sense of invulnerability: we think that individually and corporately we can live lives which are out of God's sight, far from God's reach. We get a glimpse of this in the way in which institutions and officials simply refuse accountability, refuse to acknowledge what they are and what they do or fail to do; we see it in families and workplaces where relations fall apart and people get badly hurt because no one is prepared to be honest enough to speak the truth; and we see it most closely in our own lives—we know that we lie to others, to ourselves, and to God.

Judgment—that is, *God's* judgment—is, more than anything else, God's overwhelming declaration of the truth. It's a declaration that—because it's God's—cannot be overthrown or subverted. There's no argument here, no gainsaying, no qualification or excusing. God simply says, "I know." What is it that he knows? "I know your works. You have the reputation of being alive, but you are dead" (Rev 3:1).

He knows—not appearances, reputation, the cloaks that we wrap ourselves in to evade discovery. He knows the reality of human works! And here, in this letter to Sardis, he knows that reputation and reality are very far apart indeed. The reputation is aliveness—of sharing in the life of Christ himself, of being partakers in his resurrection. The reality is utterly different: lifelessness, estrangement from the aliveness of God.

This point is worth pausing over for a moment. There are forms of apparent human aliveness that are lifeless. There are forms of apparent Christian aliveness that are also dead as dead can be. Perhaps the two most common appearances of such living death are formal religion and morality. There's a way of living the Christian life that retains its form but denies its substance. It's a form of life that can be often devoted and careful, measured, urbane, integrated, and much else. Rightly pursued, it can make quite a name for itself and acquire quite some reputation, but in the end, it can be a way of resisting God. Why? Because in the end it is utterly *safe*; for all its religious seriousness, it leaves God on the periphery; it isn't encountered, bowled over, knocked down, battered by God. It threatens to make God into simply one more interesting extension of my intact self: God without trouble, and, therefore, God without God.

The irony of it all is that what often seems to us to be a sort of human perfection is nothing of the sort. Scrupulously and carefully pursued, this kind of false aliveness indeed can seem to be perfecting human nature—the highest, the most pleasing, the finest approximation to human perfection. But here the living Christ's judgment on the whole enterprise is: No. "I have not found your works complete in the sight of my God" (Rev 3:2). The crucial thing is that little phrase "in the sight of my God." Seen from the standpoint of God's judgment, placed in the light of the word of God and the living Christ, then the work of this church—the whole enterprise of its religious and moral culture, its attempt to live out some kind of Christian life—is shown in all its imperfection. The whole thing is suddenly manifest as a failure: not perfection, but just one more episode in the sorry history of wickedness and death. And what's particularly deadly about this way of living the Christian life is the lack of readiness for encounter with Christ. Some of the most vivid and troublesome passages of the New Testament are those that look to the future coming of Christ and present a picture of the Christian life now as a matter of keeping awake at all costs, of not falling into the slumber of sin. So here: "Wake up," the angel is told (Rev 3:2). And there's an added, more potent warning: "If you will not wake up, I will come like a thief, and you will not know at what hour I will come against you" (Rev 3:3).

What we may be seeing by now is that this rather strange apocalyptic language has a pretty sharp point to make, not just to the ancient community to which it was addressed but also to us. This isn't just some sort of wild Christian explosion from the first era of the church, which can be neatly docketed as not our business. It is our business; it's talking of us and to us about who we are and who we may be. It's judgment. It's speaking about the truth of what human life is; it concerns our human lives, our evasions and half-truths and untruths. There is business for us to do with God here. For here we're pressed to do what we always must do if we're to hear and obey God: we must submit to that revolution in which God upsets and overturns our habitual thoughts about our own religious decency. We must somehow try to get hold of that most difficult of truths to grasp: that we aren't righteous, but sinners, and that we have no ground to stand before God—that *we*, of all people, may actually be alive only in name and in reality be at the point of death.

What are we to do if we're indeed to hear this word? Two things are set before this congregation in Sardis, and, therefore, before us. *First*: "Remember … what you received and heard" (Rev 3:3). That is to say, go back to the truth of the gospel. Dealing with failure and disorder in Christian discipleship is best handled by going back. That is, it's a matter of gaining a fresh grasp of the reality of our situation, which was declared to us in the proclamation of the gospel.

There is no idea here that something new is needed: some great new initiative, some fresh interpretation, something new and exciting to replace the old stuff and kickstart Christian discipleship again. Christians usually go wrong when they fail to listen to God; the remedy is to listen to God. It sounds, of course, like a terribly mundane and obvious remedy. But it is what there is. Retrospection—going back and allowing the gospel to get hold of us—is critical; there is nowhere else for us to go.

Second: "repent" (Rev 3:3). Repentance is that decisive turning of our lives that results from seeing the truth. It's the antithesis of false contentment. False contentment means simply letting things jog along, untroubled and often unaware of where we really are. False contentment uses Christian faith as a palliative, a way of numbing ourselves in just the right measure so we don't feel God too strongly but feel him just enough to ensure that we get the consolation without the affliction. Repentance, on the other hand, is what happens when we realize that God and conversion go together.

Conversion, of course, doesn't necessarily mean those dramatic events in which one way of living life is brought crashing to the ground and a new way put in its place on the spot: that's true for some but by no means for all. But for all of us, conversion means breaking free of the assumption that the straight line of my life can go on forever as it is; it means coming to see that when

God does business with me I may get torn apart in the process; it means realizing that I can and do make a mess of things and that I must take responsibility for my part of the mess; it means striding away from my sins and striding toward Christ, attentive to his word and his judgment, looking to his mercy and grace. It means agreeing with God.

This is, of course, all a bit grim, hardly the stuff to send us skipping out across the street with a light heart. But it's what's there, and we have, each of us, to make of it what we will. It's not the preacher's job to announce judgment, and it's certainly not the preacher's job to decide exactly what form that judgment will take in the lives of the poor congregation who has to listen to this sort of thing. But it is the preacher's job to try and announce what the Bible announces, and to try and say what it might mean for us if we took that announcement very seriously. Each of us has to examine himself or herself. But it's worth adding two things by way of closing.

The first is this: we can't in and of ourselves hear, or remember, or repent. We cannot do it any more than the dead can raise themselves. God must act; God the Spirit, the Creator and Renewer of human life, must make us into those who can hear God's word and can turn away from death to life. And so the basic movement of our life together, the basic movement of assembly for worship, has to be prayer for the coming of the Spirit to make us new. That, Sunday by Sunday, is the chief business of our lives.

Second, and last: the letter to Sardis ends with a promise: "The one who conquers will be clothed thus in white garments, and I will never blot his name out of the book of life. I will confess his name before my Father and before his angels" (Rev 3:5). The point of this strange language is this: there is a security for which we may properly hope. It isn't security apart from the interruptions of the gospel. It isn't security without affliction. It's the fruit of repentance and therefore a gift of grace. Above all, it's authoritative security: founded, that is, not on our perverse judgment of ourselves but on the judgment of Christ. He clothes his people with the garments of righteousness; he inscribes them on the roll of the elect; he speaks our names before the Father. Because all this is promised, then we *can* repent, hopefully and confidently. We won't lose everything if we step out of our slumber and face the truth. We will, in fact, come into the light and life of truth. And so: "He who has an ear, let him hear what the Spirit says to the churches" (Rev 3:6). Amen.

XV

THE GREAT
REVOLUTIONARY ACT

Oh give thanks to the Lord; call upon his name;
    make known his deeds among the peoples!
Sing to him, sing praises to him;
    tell of all his wondrous works!
Glory in his holy name;
    let the hearts of those who seek the Lord rejoice!
Seek the Lord and his strength;
    seek his presence continually!
Remember the wondrous works that he has done,
    his miracles, and the judgments he uttered,
O offspring of Abraham, his servant,
    children of Jacob, his chosen ones!

Psalm 105:1–6

Close to the heart of the transformation of human life, which the Christian gospel brings, is the recovery of praise. To be a Christian believer is to be converted to the praise of God. Christian faith and discipleship aren't simply a matter of acquiring a new set of beliefs nor a matter of living under a new set of moral imperatives. They certainly involve beliefs and behavior, but more fundamental than doctrine and ethics is praise. This is so because praise is the proper end of human life: it's that for which we are made.

What is it to be a human creature? Ultimately, it's to be one who praises God. Before we are rational or moral creatures, we're creatures made for praise, doxological creatures. If that is really true of us, then it means that praise of God is the supremely normal activity of human life: in it, our real humanity is expressed. What marks us out as the creatures of God isn't that we can do amazing things that other animals can't do—create language and culture and technology, make promises and break them, wage wars and forgive our enemies, and all the myriad other distinctively human activities. What marks us out is that we can glorify God, that we can glory in God's glory. We alone of all creation are appointed by God to praise and celebrate him, to call on his name, to proclaim his deeds to the nations.

What is involved is this, the original human activity? Praise isn't a single thing, and it's certainly not to be restricted to public worship, Sunday or otherwise. Praise is a cluster of activities, all of which have their center in the celebration of the sheer fact that God is God. As Psalm 105 has it, praise involves thanksgiving; it involves extolling God's mighty deeds in speech and song; it's a matter of glorying in the name of God; it involves rejoicing in the heart; it is about seeking the presence of God; and, as we praise, we remember the wonderful works of God. All of these intentions, movements, and feelings, and many more, are what make up praise. The unifying factor in all of them is that they are all aspects of what happens when human life is overtaken by a truth of such magnitude, goodness, and worthiness that we cannot but praise. And that truth is, as the psalm puts it: "He is the LORD our God" (Ps 105:7).

In all its forms, quiet or exuberant, internal or external, praise issues from our encounter with that reality: the sheer fact of God's majesty: he is the Lord. But more than that, praise flows from the realization that God's majesty is not just high over us or distant from us but turned toward us. "He is the LORD our God" (Ps 105:7): his whole being is for us, for our sake; he is the one who has pledged himself to bring about our welfare and salvation.

So, if praise has a single center, it's in the acknowledgment that God is God, and God is our God.

It's for this that we are made. The trouble is that for most of us it seems mere fantasy to speak of Christian praise in such terms. One of the most basic experiences of worship is that, far from being natural, easy, and spontaneous, welling up within us and overflowing, praise is hard, strange, and laborious. It's as if we're playing a rather unfamiliar role or wearing a suit of clothes that doesn't quite fit. Praise seems awkward and difficult. However much we may know and love the liturgical forms of praise that some of us use, all too often praise is hard, unrewarding spiritual labor. Partly it's just that we get bored or are inattentive; partly it's that we have a capacity for seemingly endless distraction. But much more, it's also that, even when we're focused and intentional, it's as if we're held back, as if we were doing something not quite easy and natural to us. Why is that? Why is it that, if God made us for praise, we seem so often to find it so terribly difficult and unsatisfying?

The answer is this: we praise God in the shadow of our fall-enness. Our praise isn't perfect and free, because we're sinners, only slowly learning to praise God. Like everything else about us, praise is caught up in the process of our being transformed by the Holy Spirit, sanctified—that is, made holy and therefore made really human. Praise is one of the things that we have to learn to do as through the grace of God we are remade, changed from rebels into God's docile and willing and obedient people. We're fallen, and so we're self-absorbed—our appetites are disorderly, our desire for God is sluggish, our delight in the things of God needs to be stimulated. We can only slowly grasp what it means to gladly acknowledge the truth about God because so much of our lives are hell-bent on repudiating that truth, or evading it, or trying to make it into something we find a bit more palatable. So praise involves toil, submitting to the process in which the warped framework of our lives is bent back into shape, reordered so that praise becomes once more our nature.

There is a very simple but extremely important practical lesson here for the way we approach worship: we need to ask God to help us praise him. Praise isn't natural—we can't just turn on the tap and let it flow. In the end, praise is something that God works in us. There's no question here of skill, of capacities that we can work on and hone to perfection. Praise is the Spirit's gift. And so the most basic prayer at the beginning of worship is this: "O Lord, open my lips, and my mouth will declare your praise" (Ps 51:15). These words aren't just a familiar bit of liturgical furniture but a cry of deepest need. They're an appeal to God that he will open our mouths though sin has made us dumb, that he will through his Spirit bestow on us the ability to praise when it's pretty much the last thing we're able and willing to do. O Lord, we pray, make haste to help us: break down our glum resistance and in your mercy make us into a people who can celebrate your glory.

So much for the nature of the praise of God to which we're called. From here, the psalm goes on to speak of two movements or activities that are fundamental to the life of praise. "Call upon his name … tell of all his wondrous works!" (Ps 105:1, 2), or, perhaps better, "make known his deeds among the peoples!" (Ps 105:1). Intrinsic to the life of praise are, first of all, invocation of God, and, second, proclamation or testimony, witness to the world about the God whom we celebrate.

First, we're commanded to call upon the name of God. Note we're *commanded* to do this. It's not an option for the believer but the most basic act of his or her life. To believe in God is to call on God's name; whatever else it may be, belief that does not call on him is just not belief in this God. Calling on God is utterly basic. And the reason for this is that calling on God corresponds to the truth of who we are. It's the primary expression of our lives as the creatures of God's grace.

What is this calling on God that is commanded? It's a confident appeal to God that looks to him as the source of all blessing. It's a turning away from self toward God, and as such it confesses two primary truths about our situation: our utter need for the grace of God, and the infinite capacity of God to provide for that need. Invoking God, calling on him in prayer, isn't an emergency measure. It's not just something that we turn to in extremity, at the hour of death or disappointment or depression. Calling on God's name accompanies all human life and all human activity when they are properly ordered. Often it takes the form of explicit, verbal prayer. At other times it may be a disposing of our lives as a whole in such a way that we acknowledge that God is our beginning and our end. But whatever form it may take, this confident appeal is, more than anything else, the real engine of human life. For people of the world, of course, it's quite simply daft—at best a consoling illusion, at worst a distraction from the real human task of making a future for ourselves. But for the people of God, it's the humble, resolute, cheerful and yet overawed acknowledgment of who we are and who God is.

Why do we invoke God? What is the basis of our confident appeal? On what grounds do we implore his merciful provision? Our calling on God is not just a shot in the dark, a cry into the void with the vague hope that we might be heard by some passing deity. It's confident, because we invoke God *by name*. The basis on which we appeal to God is his name—that is, his character as he has shown himself to be. God's name is God's revealed nature. God has made his name known—that is, he has manifested to us who he is. And at the core of that "naming," at the heart of this self-revealing, is the demonstration that God is merciful. We call on his name as Creator who brought us into being. We call on his name as Reconciler who has destroyed sin and death and made life to triumph. We call on his name as Redeemer who pledges to bring our lives to glory. It's the God who is and does these things whom we invoke; above all, it's the God who names himself as the God and Father of our Lord Jesus Christ. To call on this God, in the name of Jesus and in the power of the Spirit, is to ask with certainty for grace, forgiveness, peace, joy, and healing, and thereby to fulfill our human vocation.

Calling on God's name is an inward movement that flows from praise of God. Corresponding to that movement is another, external movement, the movement of declaration. "Make known his deeds among the peoples!" (Ps 105:1). If the people of God form a community of praise, and if that praise engenders invocation of God, we're no less a community of witness. Praise and prayer issue in proclamation to the nations. In the same way that Israel wasn't for itself but a light for the world, so also the church is directed to the whole earth, to all humanity. Because our praise is for the sake of God, it's therefore for the sake of the world. What does this mean?

Authentic praise is never simply turned in on itself. Praise is a sign set up in the world. Praise and prayer testify to a different, new, wholly unexpected thing—they draw attention to the fact that God is making the world new. The church's praise and prayer are the acknowledgment of the converting and healing presence of God, and that acknowledgment sends its shock waves through the whole world. It's a very strange thing in our culture to do what we do day by day, Sunday by Sunday in this place. We gather together and praise God in speech and song. We try to listen to the word of God and ponder what it may be that God says to us. We beseech him for forgiveness and help; we ask him to have mercy on our world and secure its future. Because we do all this quietly, tucked away inside our places of worship and pretty much invisible to all but those who bother to seek us out, the temptation is to think that it's all a sort of private affair, without much public significance. But no! The worship of God is not something we cultivate as an arcane, specialist activity, something for a few connoisseurs. It's a great revolutionary act.

When we praise God, when we invoke his name, we say "no" to sin and death; we turn our backs on human chaos; we reject the sullenness with which sin refuses to call on God. And we thereby set up a sign in the world which—simply by keeping going with praise and prayer—points the world to the truth of its redemption. Therefore one test of the genuineness of our worship will be whether it is genuinely declaratory. By "declaratory" I do not mean noisy or aggressive or culturally strident. I mean this: Does our praise of God resist the temptation to revolve on itself and instead display to the world that in God alone is its true health and salvation?

All of this is to say that the praise of God is close to the center of the church's mission in the world. One of the chief ways in which the church sets the gospel before the world is by sticking to its post, fulfilling the command of God to praise him, invoke his name, and thereby declare his deeds. It's precisely this—apparently so irrelevant, so marginal, so ineffectual—which is the point at which the church moves against the world's self-sufficiency. Churches often struggle to be relevant and are sometimes tempted to go overboard, casting themselves around in a frenzy to catch up with the latest bits of cultural hardware and so engage the world on its own terms. But really, engaging the world means doing the one thing which no one else does: praising the Lord Jesus and announcing the gospel concerning him. This doesn't mean we're called to be deliberately isolationist or sectarian, but it does mean that our mission in the world must involve learning to sing the songs of Zion even if no one seems to be listening—for soon enough, we'll discover that they are listening and that the songs of Zion declare the world's healing like nothing else.

What the psalm therefore asks us to mull over is a question concerning this great work that God commands us to undertake and to which we have pledged ourselves—namely, the service of God and God's world in praise and prayer. In the first letter of Peter, this is said of us: "You are a chosen race, a royal priesthood, a holy nation, a people for his own possession" (1 Pet 2:9a); and why? "That you may proclaim the excellencies of him who called you out of darkness into his marvelous light" (1 Pet 2:9b). You don't need to be a mind reader to know that there are lots of people around who more than anything else need light. The miracle of the gospel is that God, in his mercy, has caused his light to shine, and it's the task of God's people to order their praises in such a way that they indicate his presence and glory: to whom be glory, now and for ever. Amen.

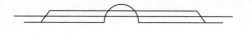

PART IV

SALVATION'S VIRTUES

XVI

WISDOM

Solomon loved the Lord, walking in the statutes of David his father, only he sacrificed and made offerings at the high places. And the king went to Gibeon to sacrifice there, for that was the great high place. Solomon used to offer a thousand burnt offerings on that altar. At Gibeon the Lord appeared to Solomon in a dream by night, and God said, "Ask what I shall give you." And Solomon said, "You have shown great and steadfast love to your servant David my father, because he walked before you in faithfulness, in righteousness, and in uprightness of heart toward you. And you have kept for him this great and steadfast love and have given him a son to sit on his throne this day. And now, O Lord my God, you have made your servant king in place of David my father, although I am but a little child. I do not know how to go out or come in. And your servant is in the midst of your people whom you have chosen, a great people, too many to be numbered or counted for multitude. Give your servant therefore an understanding mind to govern your people, that I may discern between good and evil, for who is able to govern this your great people?"

1 Kings 3:3–9

Most of us, I think, have a conventional idea of what it means to be a wise person. We ordinarily think of wisdom as a frame of mind that helps us pierce to the truth about the people, situations, and problems that demand our attention. Wisdom involves going through the externals to the deep things underneath. The person without wisdom is mesmerized by surfaces and is either too lazy or too distracted to do anything other than take everything at face value. The wise person waits, and probes, and so sees things that ordinarily would escape us because we are in too much of a rush to notice. Wisdom is a kind of stability; the wise, we say, are steady as a rock, unflustered, not buffeted about by images (or "spin" as they say nowadays); the wise have a settled temper that helps them discern.

I suppose that's one of the reasons why wisdom is so little valued these days in the public sphere. We find ourselves sadly in a vulgar and opinionated culture in which taking one's time, thinking and speaking slowly, are largely despised. The price we pay is that wisdom gets pushed to the margins, and so truth gets sacrificed, for it's the office of the wise to see, to perceive, and so to help us both know and act out the truth.

Christian people will find little to quarrel with in that understanding of wisdom and lots they want to affirm. Nevertheless, there's something very distinctive about how Christians are to think about the nature of human wisdom. If our thinking is properly guided by Scripture, then we are led to say something like this: wisdom is God's gift. Wisdom isn't something we can acquire by the exercise of our own powers, however noble those powers may be. If we seek to make ourselves wise, if we look to our own resources, then not only will we fail to catch wisdom; we will become fools, those who are deaf to the instruction of the Lord. In short, it is God who makes wise; it is God who gives discernment of good and evil.

If that's true, then it already strikes at the heart of one of our most cherished illusions about ourselves. That illusion is the foolish idea that human wisdom is the natural product of experience and reflection. We're often tempted to think that wisdom just grows with age, that acquiring wisdom is a matter of ordinary human maturing. Or, again, sometimes we're tempted to believe that we can make ourselves wise—that if we practice hard and often enough, if we build the right virtues and habits into our lives, if we work at it, we can somehow cultivate wisdom. But to this kind of cultivated wisdom, this wisdom that we can nurture and grow, the word of God says a pretty firm "no." And it says no because the whole business of acquiring wisdom out of our own resources is folly and, indeed, worse than folly: it is a repetition of the very core of human sin. For at the heart of sin is a refusal to be instructed by God.

The essence of human rebellion against God, the essence of human fallenness, is a refusal to let God tell us the difference between good and evil. Sin is the folly of thinking that, apart from God and by exercising our best powers of mind and conscience, we can master the distinction between good and evil. Why is that sin? Because—as the serpent in the garden of Eden puts it with devastating clarity—it makes us gods. It puts us in the position where knowing the difference between good and evil is no longer a gift but a power. Wisdom is no longer a matter of prayer, of looking to God, but a matter of human judgment. It's not first and foremost a hearing, but a speaking. It's therefore for all its urbane exterior a kind of perversity, a refusal to be creatures. And that's why God will destroy the wisdom of the wise—that is, God's decision about the whole sorry process of human production and acquisition of wisdom is that it must be reduced to rubble if we're ever to become truly wise.

All of which takes us to Solomon and his prayer. What may we learn from his prayer about the true character of wisdom and the true place where it may be found? Very simply, we may learn this: that it is God who gives "a wise and discerning mind" (1 Kgs 3:12), and that wisdom is, therefore, that for which we must pray. Solomon prayed: "Give your servant therefore an understanding mind" (1 Kgs 3:9).

Wisdom, discernment, truly understanding the truth, is a gift, not a possession. We don't produce it, we don't handle it or manage it: God gives. When God gives, God doesn't, as it were, hand over the gift to us for our control, for us to do with it as we will, for us to turn it into something that henceforth we own and can control as we wish. God's gifts always retain their character as gift, even as God gives them; gifts are events of giving, not commodities handed over to us. And so when we are given the gift of wisdom and discernment, it doesn't mean that henceforth we own wisdom, that we've now come to possess what God used to possess but which we can now exercise without reference to God. The wise person isn't an owner of wisdom but always the recipient of God's gift of wisdom, ever afresh taking it from the hands of God, who is alone wise.

This means two things. It means, first, of all that at the heart of wisdom is a sense of our inability to be wise on our own. Sometimes our picture of the wise person is of someone firm, steady, authoritative, assured in their judgments. But for Scripture, wisdom is the opposite of assurance. Wisdom is born of not knowing, not trusting our own capacity. We begin to be wise not when we trust how much we know, how much experience we've accumulated, but when we acknowledge that we know nothing, that we're never been anything other than beginners, that we need to be taught afresh. "I am but a little child," says Solomon (1 Kgs 3:7). For him, the cultivation of wisdom is pointless, a sheer impossibility; all that lies in him, as in everyone of us, is unfittingness, unreadiness, incapacity. The fear of the Lord is the beginning of wisdom. Fearing God means realizing just how utterly impossible it is to bridge the gulf between God and us; fearing God involves us in self-distrust; it means that in wisdom, as in all things, we can only proceed in fear and trembling, because all things come from the hands of God alone.

This is why, second, at the heart of wisdom is a prayer for wisdom. Solomon prayed. Solomon prayed because he was a creature and, as a creature, needed the grace of God. If he was to discern right and wrong, if he was to be able to see the truth, then he had to go to God and ask. We don't therefore tell a wise person by their sententious judgments or their gravity; we tell a wise person by their prayers, by their sense that without God they have no adequacy at all. "If anyone imagines that he knows something," Paul reminds us, "he does not yet know as he ought to know" (1 Cor 8:2). But we don't know, we can't discern—and so we pray. John Calvin once said that the real mark of the wise is this: they are "poor, empty, void of self-wisdom: eager to learn but knowing nothing." I think he got it right!

What then should we do? Maybe Ephesians may help: "Look carefully then how you walk," the author exhorts us, "not as unwise but as wise" (Eph 5:15). But how do we do that? Not by training alone; not by learning alone; not by the refinement of our moral sensibilities—however much God may be pleased to sanctify these things if he will. No: we walk as the wise by being "filled with the Spirit" (Eph 5:18). Being filled with the Spirit means, very simply, being united to Jesus Christ by the Spirit's power.

The Spirit-filled person is the one who has been knocked out of the center of their own life, who has been displaced by Jesus Christ, so that it is Christ who lives in that person. One of the Spirit's gifts is wisdom—and for that gift we must therefore pray.

We do not gather in church worship to celebrate our achievements or advertise our piety, good taste, moral uprightness, or, indeed, our wisdom. We gather because there are things we need, desperately, and only God can supply us with what we need. We need forgiveness; we need to be healed from our resistance to the truth; we need help to make our cold hearts and wills spring to life; like Solomon, we need to discern what is right. God alone is our help. And so we pray:

> O God, who art near to all that call upon thee in truth; who art thyself the truth, whom to know is eternal life: Instruct us with thy divine wisdom, and teach us thy law, that we may know the truth and walk in it; through him in whom the truth was made manifest, thy Son Jesus Christ our Lord. Amen.

XVII

COURAGE

HAVE I not commanded you? Be strong and courageous. Do not be frightened, and do not be dismayed, for the Lord your God is with you wherever you go.

JOSHUA 1:9

BE strong in the Lord and in the strength of his might.

EPHESIANS 6:10

What does the Christian gospel have to teach us about the virtue of courage? Courage, we may say by way of beginning, is the capacity to face and overcome fear. As such, it's an aspect of what might be called strength in human character. Strength of character involves, among other things, the capacity to resist impulses, desires, and emotions so that we aren't ruled by them. Those who we acknowledge to be strong are those who aren't deflected from the purpose or end of their lives by obstacles. They aren't stopped in their course by hindrances or distracted by whatever comes to hand. They are steadfast, as Ephesians puts it; they are people who withstand, and, having done all, are still standing (Eph 6:11, 13–14). And one of the ways in which we talk about this firmness of character is courage.

Courage isn't an isolated matter but is very closely related to a cluster of other human virtues. It's related to self-control, in which we make sure that desires and appetites don't run away with us; it's close to patience, in which we handle the adversities of tedium and irritation; it's close, also, to perseverance, in which we keep going despite discouragement at the apparent fruitlessness of our lives. But courage has a particular task to perform: *it is the particular business of courage to face fear*—to encounter those things and people and situations that make us afraid and to not be crushed or overwhelmed by them. In courage, we face the dread that is generated in us by outward circumstances or inner state (by physical threats, or pain, or worry, or loss of honor and reputation), and we do not allow it to knock us off course. It's with courage that martyrs go to their deaths, choosing to face the terror of death rather than deny the truth; for us more prosaic mortals, it's courage that has to accompany us into the operating theater or the interview room.

Courage is only really courage when it is strength of character directed to a good and noble end. Merely acting purposefully in face of fearful danger isn't in and of itself courage. Thieves, seducers, and terrorists can appear to be courageous, risking all manner of menaces to attain their goals. But facing and overcoming danger for a worthless and wicked cause isn't courage. Courage is only true courage when it's enlisted in the service of truth and goodness. Sheer force of purpose, sheer tenacity, isn't enough. Nor is courage just rashness or daredevilry. The courageous person doesn't enjoy danger or seek it out for purposes of self-display. Deliberately courting danger for the sake of demonstrating one's capacity to confront a threat isn't courage but folly and ostentation. The truly courageous person doesn't seek out opportunities for the exercise of strength of character. Rather, courage is evoked when we face something which we can't avoid: the fear which can arise as part of following a good purpose or from unavoidable misfortune.

What is involved in the exercise of courage? Courage, we might say, faces fear and isn't turned aside from pursuing what we know to be good and true. When we're courageous, we do what is right even though doing so makes us afraid. If this is so, then courage involves a lot more than just willpower; it's not simply sheer doggedness or determination. Courage involves a firm sense of who we are and of the kind of world we live in. It flows from a clear and coherent sense of our identity. Courageous people are people who have attained to a well-defined sense of what it means for them to be them. A person with an insecure or unformed sense of themselves will find courage acutely difficult and so may often be overtaken by fear. A person whose sense of themselves is more deeply rooted will be more likely to act purposefully in the face of fear. And, what is more, the courageous person will usually be a person who has attained a firm sense of what sort of place the world is. Above all, men and women of courage believe that the world is the kind of place in which courageous action is possible and truthful, in which fear isn't the last word. The courageous know fear; they may at times be sick at heart. But, despite everything, they aren't intimidated or reduced to nothing, because the world is not only full of danger but also a place in which courage will make a difference.

All that is to say that courage requires a measure of clarity and assurance about ourselves and about the world. But where do those things come from? It's here that our readings from Scripture begin to instruct us. "Be strong and courageous. Do not be frightened, and do not be dismayed, for the LORD your God is with you wherever you go," God says to Joshua; "Be strong in the Lord and in the strength of his might," the writer of Ephesians says to his readers (Josh 1:9; Eph 6:10). Let's begin from Joshua.

Here he is, Moses' long-standing second-in-command, who now finds himself at the head of a restless and pretty chaotic group of long-term migrants—an assorted group, which has just lost its leader and is poised on the brink of a great episode in its history in which it will have to battle to establish itself or perish. This group now faces all sorts of acute threats: internal disorder, external attack, and the persistent desire to ease difficulties by compromising the will of God. In that dire set of circumstances,

Joshua is exhorted to exercise courage. But, notice, the courage to which he is exhorted isn't mere wild daring; it's a courage which faces and overcomes fear because to do so is truthful; it's therefore a courage that is rooted in the way the world really is, in the deep truth of Joshua's situation and the situation of all the people of God.

What is this deep truth? This: that, despite the fact that the world is full of terrors and threats for which Joshua is utterly inadequate, despite the fact that his heart will melt like wax when he faces what he must face, nevertheless one thing stands: "... the LORD your God is with you wherever you go" (Josh 1:9). If Joshua is called to courage, it's to a courage fixed upon the presence of God. That presence entails two things.

First, *God's presence is the presence of the one who is establishing his purpose for his people.* God says to Joshua: "Moses my servant is dead. Now therefore arise, go over this Jordan, you and all this people, into the land that I am giving to them, to the people of Israel" (Josh 1:2). The people of Israel are conquering a land that has already been purposed for them and given to them by God: "You shall cause this people to inherit the land that I swore to their fathers to give them" (Josh 1:6). The land is inherited, not annexed or taken over. Israel is entering into the divine allotment.

That's a hard thought for us in the light of the present-day agonies of Israel and Palestine. But the point for now is: Joshua can be exhorted to be of good courage and to not fail in his purpose, not because everything rests on his shoulders, not because he must be courageous in order to win. Quite the opposite: the ground of his courage is the promise of God. Without that promise, without the divine gift of the new land, courage would be at best self-assertion and at worst moral evil. The courage that Joshua is called to exercise is courage in face of the fact that God is already moving through the history of the world. Fear can, therefore, be faced resolutely because there is that which lies on the other side of fear—namely, a prosperity that lies in the hands of God alone, which God pledges by his presence. To be courageous isn't a venture, a wager against fate; it's that to which Joshua is called by a sober realization that God is with his people.

Second, therefore: *for Joshua, God's presence is the presence of one who appoints him to a specific task and equips him for that task.* How can Joshua follow the divine bidding and "arise"? How can he lift up his heart? How, above all, can he replace Moses, the Lord's servant? The answer lies in the divine commission that Joshua has received. Joshua stands in the same presence and under the same promise as Moses himself. "Just as I was with Moses, so I will be with you. I will not leave you or forsake you" (Josh 1:5). Courage comes from a sense of the divine call, for God's call focuses and directs the life of the one who is called. And as it does so, the call of God takes from us that overwhelming sense of responsibility, that crushing sense in which everything depends upon our capacities.

When we speak of God's call, we speak of the way in which God appoints us to be and do certain things, and, moreover, we are saying that God makes us into people who *can* be and do these things. As God calls, so God equips; God's commissioning is also God's enabling. To be called isn't to be dragged into the ring resourceless, alone, and told to fight. It's to be called to act in God's presence, a presence that is infinitely resourceful, infinitely reliable: "I will be with you. I will not leave you or forsake you" (Josh 1:5).

God's presence doesn't abolish fear or the things that generate fear. But it does say this: like Joshua, the people of God keep company with God. The world is the place where God is, and so it's a place where it makes sense to be exhorted, "Be strong and courageous" (Josh 1:9).

Perhaps we can begin to see that there is instruction for us here about the way in which we ourselves are to exercise courage as the followers of Jesus Christ. Courage has its basis in something about God: *that God is God with us.* So, as we find in the passage from Ephesians that we read, Christians are called to "be strong *in the Lord*"; the strength with which they encounter fear and danger is "the strength of his might" (Eph 6:10).

The courageous Christian, like Joshua, is courageous because of the promise and reality of God's protection. Courage is enabled by the security afforded by what Ephesians calls the "armor of God"; fear can be met because we know ourselves to be shielded by his reality. And so there is a proper cheerfulness and confidence and, indeed, lack of care in Christian courage—not a foolhardy contempt for danger but a prudent and happy sense that danger isn't the only thing there is. Fear will not master us, because in the midst of knowing fear we also know the reality of God and the gospel. God in Christ in the Spirit's power is with us and for us; we are "in the Lord." And in that we're safe; by that we can be courageous.

The courageous Christian knows these things. But he or she knows these things not by nature nor just by miraculous and momentary persuasion but because they've been learned. And they're learned by long training, by practice, by the shaping of a life into bravery. How can this be done? How can we acquire the habit of courageously facing fear and overcoming?

In the book of Joshua, the answer to those questions lies in life under the instruction of the law of God.

> Only be strong and very courageous, being careful to do according to all the law that Moses my servant commanded you. Do not turn from it to the right hand or to the left, that you may have good success wherever you go. This Book of the Law shall not depart from your mouth, but you shall meditate on it day and night, so that you may be careful to do according to all that is written in it. For then you will make your way prosperous, and then you will have good success. (Josh 1:7–8)

The law here is not just a code of regulations, a set of arbitrary rules. Law is the revealed purpose of God for God's creatures.

Through the law we're led to our flourishing, for it teaches what it is to be human and what it means to fulfill our natures. The end of the law is what is here called "success" or "prospering": full humanity, humanity fulfilled.

Living under the law involves a number of attitudes and practices. It involves attentiveness, being careful and stable in our observance and not lacking in diligence. It involves a certain directedness, resisting our desire to be free of its bonds. It involves meditating upon it, making it a matter for the heart and the mind and so shaping the affections and the will. Keeping the law in this way isn't at all a matter of craven obedience; it's very far from inhibited and anxious scruple. It's a way of being shaped by the truth so that we grow in fellowship with God. And in that fellowship with God, overseen by the law, we may grow into courage and so be set free from fear.

For Christian people, this being shaped by the law is also a matter of being shaped by the gospel. We're to live in the gospel's light; the gospel alone is to govern our hearts and our attachments, to determine our wills and so quicken us to action. Where do we find the gospel? We hear it in holy Scripture. It's portrayed to us in the sacraments. It is lived out in the life of faith in the fellowship of the church. Like all the virtues, courage grows as we live a life in which those things—Scripture, sacraments, faith, fellowship—are deeply and permanently important. Only so may we be strong in the Lord.

Courage will be required of most of us at some point in our lives; it will be required of all us at our death. We do not know in advance the occasions when we will be called upon to exercise courage. What we do know is that we must learn now to steady our spirits, to learn of God, to govern our lives by the gift of his presence, so that when we ourselves are told to arise and be of good courage, we may heed God's call.

May God give us grace to ponder these things, to his glory and to our great and endless comfort. Amen.

XVIII

THANKFULNESS

WE give thanks to God always for all of you, constantly mentioning you in our prayers, remembering before our God and Father your work of faith and labor of love and steadfastness of hope in our Lord Jesus Christ.

1 THESSALONIANS 1:2–3

Like nearly all the other letters of Paul that we have in the New Testament canon, 1 Thessalonians starts with thanksgiving. It's relatively easy to breeze through these sections of thanksgiving at the beginning of Paul's letters without really paying attention to the fact that something of importance is happening in them. All too easily we can think of them as just courtesies that Paul goes through before getting on with the real business of his letters, or perhaps we may read them as if Paul were engaging in a bit of flattery, winning his readers over before he has a go at them on some issue that's troubling him. But if we pause over them and ponder a little, we soon come to see that something else is going on.

Far from being mere civil preliminaries, these introductory thanksgivings tell us something very profound. They signal to us the kind of existence in which both Paul and his readers are caught up. Paul gives thanks because, for him, Christian life, life in Christ and life in the church of Christ, is a life in which thanksgiving is a fundamental dynamic. Thanksgiving isn't just decoration; it's primary. Basic to the whole pattern of living in which Paul and his readers share is the giving and receiving of thanks.

Thanksgiving in the church of Jesus Christ is a deep reality. It's not just a sign that Christians are a well-mannered lot who say nice things about one another and are suitably grateful to God for their blessings. Thanksgiving is one of the signs of convertedness— that is, it's a mark of the fact that those who live in Christ have been remade, transplanted out of one way of living into another, new way. This is because, as Paul puts it, the gospel has come to them in power and the Holy Spirit. Because they have turned to God from idols—because under the impulse of God they have abandoned an entire way of living—their mode of existence has been turned inside-out. One of the essential aspects of that conversion and renewal of human life is the move from ingratitude to thanksgiving.

Christian life is new life because it transforms us out of our refusal to live thankfully to a life which acknowledges, celebrates, and lives from the grace of God. Part of what makes the church such a strange reality in the world is that it's a place where callousness and ingratitude are being set aside and human beings are beginning to learn one of the fundamental things we must learn if we are to be healed—namely, how to say those words which can chase away an entire army of demons: *we give thanks to God always*.

So thanksgiving is one of the chief fruits of that complete reorientation of human life that Christian faith is all about: to be in the church is to rediscover gratitude to God. Thanksgiving is thus rooted in grace: to live in gratitude to God is to live out of God's grace. And grace is not a thing but a person and an action. It's the personal presence and action of God; it's God giving to us wretched and convoluted creatures everything we need to rescue us from our wretchedness and set our lives straight.

Who is this grace-filled God whose goodness sets us free for thanksgiving? For Paul in 1 Thessalonians, it is God who is Father, Son, and Spirit, the merciful three-in-one. The God who sets us free for thanksgiving is, Paul tells us, "God the Father" or "our

God and Father"; he is "the Lord Jesus Christ," equal to him in majesty and grace; and he is God "the Holy Spirit," the life-giver. This God, in his threefold work of grace, is the one who comes to us in his great act of friendship, wiping out our sins, reconciling us to himself, restoring us to fellowship, and setting us free to be who we are made to be: *God's thankful people.*

Gratitude, we might say, echoes grace; the giving of thanks flows from God's supreme gift of fellowship with himself. But notice that thanksgiving has not only a vertical but also a horizontal dimension. Paul gives thanks not only for God's work of salvation but also for the way in which God's grace spills over into the lives of his fellow believers.

The grace of God overflows and transforms, making human lives new, making them flourish in fresh and unexpected ways. It breaks up the hard ground of human sin, and good things begin to appear, graces and virtues that we never thought to see. When the gospel goes to work in human life, all sorts of noble and excellent things start happening, and these in turn become further matter for that ceaseless activity of giving thanks to God, which is the basic activity of the Christian life. So here with Paul: he looks upon his fellow servants of Jesus Christ as something very specific—as an occasion and cause of thanksgiving: "We give thanks to God always for all of you" (1 Thess 1:2).

What does Paul give thanks for? He gives thanks for the fact that in the lives of this little group of believers he sees some things which are startlingly new and the manifestations of human life brought back from the dead. And what he sees are that familiar triplet of gospel virtues—namely faith, love, and hope. Notice that Paul gives thanks to *God* for their presence. These human excellences aren't exhibitions of the moral or spiritual capacities of the people who exercise them. They're the signs of grace. If there is faith, love, and hope among these Thessalonian Christians, it's because and only because they're the fruit of God's inspiring presence and action—because in the power of the risen Christ and with the energy of the Holy Spirit, God's grace makes them possible.

But grace does not mean the end of human work. Faith, love, and hope aren't only what God's grace makes possible; they're what human beings really *do*. Paul speaks of "your *work* of faith and *labor* of love and *steadfastness* of hope" (1 Thess 1:3). It's not, of course, work or labor or steadfastness independent of God's grace; it's work and labor and steadfastness empowered and sustained by God. But what God empowers and sustains is our active life: God makes it possible for us to act humanly.

God makes possible, first, the "work of faith." That is, God makes possible the kind of life that is the outworking of faith. In a deep sense faith is not a human "work"; it's receiving and trusting in God's work, and it's generated by God's Spirit. But as faith trusts in God and God's ways and purposes, so faith is set to work. In faith we're set free to work—not in order to win God's favor or prove to ourselves that we're good, but as the natural expression of trust in the fact that God has remade the world and called us to live in the truth.

Second, God makes possible the "labor of love." Nowadays by that phrase we usually mean unrewarded hard work, but here Paul means engaging in the struggle to build up and maintain common human life. He means that those who have faith in God are committed to the task of fellowship: living in company with the others whom God has given us. That task is laborious because it inevitably involves all sorts of discouragement and opposition, from other people and from ourselves, and it's all too easy to shirk the task as just too troublesome. But Paul here gives thanks that his hearers haven't given up on themselves or one another but have persevered and made the church into a place of genuine human reconciliation, a place of fellowship.

Third, God makes possible "steadfastness of hope." The works of faith and the labor of love involve real drudgery: the unromantic and usually invisible business of keeping going without too much by way of reward and with few spectacular successes. To keep going, people need hope: they need a sense that there really is a direction to life, that all those little steps of faith and love are going somewhere. "Steadfast hope" is about active, persistent, enduring commitment to keeping going—not just out of dogged-ness, but out of a sense that our work isn't pointless but has its end in one thing: the Lord Jesus Christ. His coming, his presence, and his vindication gather up our works and give them a goal that sustains us when the only thing we want to do is to give up.

Such acts of faith, love, and hope build up the church's fellowship. They do so in two ways. First, they're the occasions for the church exercising thanksgiving, and thanksgiving nourishes the community: it's a good and wholesome activity that cements common life. Thanksgiving liberates us from self-preoccupation and helps us live in true freedom, the freedom of grace. Second, when that happens, when the church becomes a thankful community, then our attitude to our neighbors in Christ is transformed. How? Because our neighbors in the church present us not with a threat or an opportunity to criticize or a matter of contempt but with God's grace at work. They indicate the traces of the risen Jesus Christ himself among us; they indicate the Holy Spirit active in transforming power.

We aren't talking here of great miracles but of seemingly little things—of the faith that trusts God and so presses ahead with a project when the tide is running against us; of the love that keeps patience with our difficult colleagues or relatives and doesn't give up on them; of the hope that is not deterred by discouragement. We must ask God to help us in our small way to exercise these things and so make us a cause of thanksgiving to our neighbors in Christ. And this will take us close to the heart of the gospel.

I hope people don't get weary of my quotations from Calvin, but this one is too good to miss. Commenting on these verses of Paul, Calvin finds in them "a brief definition of true Christianity," which he says, is this: "It is an earnest faith, full of power, so that it shirks no task when our neighbors are in need of help. ... The godly are all to be strenuously occupied in duties of love, and on these to spend their energies. Intent on the hope of the manifes-tation of Christ they are to despise all other things and armed with patience to rise superior to both wearisome delay and the temptations of the world."

> We give thanks to God always for all of you, constantly mentioning you in our prayers, remembering before our God and Father your work of faith and labor of love and steadfastness of hope in our Lord Jesus Christ. (1 Thess 1:2–3)

> Amen.

XIX

GENEROSITY

FOR you know the grace of our Lord Jesus Christ, that
though he was rich, yet for your sake he became poor, so
that you by his poverty might become rich.

2 CORINTHIANS 8:9

I want us to think a little together about Christian generosity.
When we think about a virtue like generosity, we can often
fall into a trap. The trap is thinking that we already know what
generosity is, because generosity is something that most people
seem to have some basic grasp of and which a lot of people also
manage to put into practice now and again. If we think like that—if
we think that there's nothing specifically *Christian* about Christian
generosity—then all that preachers need to do is provide a bit of
an incentive: exhort, admonish, and otherwise persuade people
that this natural human duty is one at which the church of Jesus
Christ also needs to work.

For Paul in 2 Corinthians, however, things are very different.
Generosity is one of the deep and holy things of the gospel;
it's to be understood not just as a civic virtue for all people
of good will but as an obligation and delight that flows from
the good news of salvation; it's one of the signs of the radical
reorientation of our social lives that arises from life in Christ.
In thinking about generosity, then, we're not just in the realm
of money management and charitable giving; we're in the realm

of the miracle of God's lavish, life-giving, and saving work among us in Jesus Christ.

The passage from 2 Corinthians that we're looking at is a little fragment of a larger story, and the larger story goes something like this: in the mid 50s of the first century, one of Paul's major projects was organizing a collection from the various Christian communities with which he had contact as an aid package for the Jewish Christians in Jerusalem. The Jerusalem church was suffering acute hardship: already composed of poorer folk, it was in no state to ride easily through the economic downturn afflicting that part of the world. For Paul, a collection to relieve the needs of these Jewish Christians was not only a fitting expression of gratitude on the part of gentile Christians to their Jewish spiritual benefactors, it was also a manifestation of a basic truth of the gospel—namely, the unity of the church in Christ. So he got a collection going, and, among others, the church at Corinth got involved.

The Corinthian end of things seems to have been handled by Titus. It appears that the system was a weekly collection taken on the Lord's Day, with people offering according to their abilities; the collection was to be stored up and then eventually sent to Jerusalem. However, Paul and the Corinthian church fell out rather drastically: he criticized their immoral behavior in no uncertain terms, and they gave as good as they took, thinking he was throwing around his weight as an apostle. By the time that 2 Corinthians came to be written, things seem to have been largely patched up, and Paul tries to get the collection moving again. To do so, he sets before the Corinthians the example of the Macedonian churches, who seem to have provided a startling example of Christian generosity, and he appeals to the Corinthians to do likewise.

What's important about the incident, and what gives it abiding significance for us, is the way in which Paul understands the generosity for which he is calling. For him, the practice of generosity isn't just a matter of disposing of spare cash sensibly in order to help others; rather, it points us toward the heart of the gospel and the character of God's acts, which the gospel declares. There are four matters in particular that we might ponder along these lines.

First: *at the root of Christian generosity is the generosity of God himself.* In telling the Corinthians about how the Christians in Macedonia had responded, he says: "We want you to know, brothers, about the grace of God that has been given among the churches of Macedonia" (2 Cor 8:1).

Notice what he's doing. As he draws the attention of his hearers to what others are about in order to stimulate their action, he begins from a very particular point. He doesn't start by talking about the efforts or piety or self-sacrifice or commitment of these folk. He starts with *the grace of God.* That is, if there is a readiness and openhandedness in Macedonia, if there's an example to which Paul can appeal, then at its heart is the work of God himself.

The remarkable generosity of these Macedonians isn't some sort of human attainment: it comes from the grace of God that has been given to them. In short: over and above the gift that they give to others, there is an unsurpassably greater gift that they have received from the hands of God himself.

Christian generosity flows from the generosity of God. It does so in two ways. First of all, God himself acts with generosity—God acts with "grace." The lives of these Macedonian and Corinthian Christians, and of all Christians, are what they are because God is gracious—because God in his mercy has not left the world to suffer in its misery and ruin but has come to the world and its people, lent them his aid, and rescued them from their distress. Second, in acting with grace, in acting out the divine generosity, God makes our generosity possible. God's abundant generosity makes it possible for us, too, to put an end to hardness of heart and refusal to hear our neighbors' cry for help and instead to become those who don't just receive God's generosity but also pass on that generosity to others. The miracle of God's grace is echoed in the human grace that it makes possible.

All this, of course, makes very clear once again that Christian generosity is a great deal more than just Christians parting with their cash, their time, or whatever else they are asked to give. Christian generosity in incomprehensible apart from receiving and living from and extending the mercy of God. It comes not from the natural heart, unschooled by the gospel, but from that transformation of all human life and all human action which we call the grace of God.

Second, therefore: *generosity is abundance and overflow in the midst of affliction and poverty*. What Paul really wants to draw attention to in the Macedonian Christians is this: in a severe test of affliction, their abundance of joy and their extreme poverty have overflowed in a wealth of liberality.

What does he mean? Well, we do know that these Macedonian churches had hit very hard times themselves. Though at that time Macedonia was a flourishing area, Christians there faced persecution and, in particular, exclusion from public life and from most means of trade. And so they found themselves right at the bottom of the economic pile: confession of Christ meant the end of material well-being. But, crucially, such affliction and poverty did not suppress their generosity. Quite the opposite: it quickened it and made them overflow in liberality. Because their lives were lived from the grace of God and in response to the grace of God, their sufferings didn't mean they closed themselves off from others; instead, affliction led to abundant generosity, and they begged for the favor of taking part in the relief of the saints.

How on earth can we understand this strange business of the afflicted and impoverished showing themselves to be the model of generosity? For Paul, these things cannot be explained any other way than by the reality of God and the gospel of God's grace. For there is that about God, and that about the Christian gospel, which concerns extravagance, abundance, and overflowing generosity. In particular, there is that about God and about the Christian gospel which overthrows one of our most instinctive and powerful responses to affliction and material hardship. The first casualty in hardship is generosity. Why? Because it's fatally easy in hard material circumstances to be overtaken by the need to possess—to hang on, to secure our fragile lives by keeping a firm grip on such material things as we can call our own. Only in that way, we are tempted to think we can keep our status; only through property can we have our dignity and safety from attack. All this is, of course, entirely understandable: it's human nature. But it's not quite the way of the gospel, because the gospel reverses our natural self-protection.

The gospel declares to us and offers to us the free gift of life—a life that we have not earned or built up out of our own resources, a life that we don't need to hang on to at all costs, because it's ours in God, by God's gift of grace. And because the gospel is about that gift of God, it abolishes the need to possess, to build up a wall of property around ourselves. Because the gospel is true, then we're set free to do what Paul says these Macedonian Christians are doing—to live beyond our means. The good news of God's lavish goodness toward us sets us free from the cramp that afflicts us when we hold on to our property. The gospel announces that God has delivered us from possession and freed us for joy, for liberality, and for excess. Through Jesus Christ—through the one who is God's generosity in person—we have been released to live generously with the saints.

Third, *Christian generosity involves fellowship and service.* Tucked away in 2 Corinthians 8:4 are two key ideas. They're a bit obscured in the translation we used. That verse is really saying something like this: "The Macedonian Christians begged earnestly for the grace of fellowship in the service of the saints." What are this fellowship and this service that comprise the elements of generosity?

First of all, fellowship. The church of Jesus Christ is a collection of those who are brought together by a miracle. That miracle is the generosity of God, the abundant overflow of God's mercy. It's a miracle that gathers a people around itself: brought together by the astonishing reality of God's grace, the people of the church live in a double fellowship. They have a common share in the riches of God's salvation—their fellowship is their common participation in the treasures of grace—forgiveness, peace with God, freedom, calling, hope. They also have a common life: because they are bound to God's salvation, they are also bound to each other.

That means that the people of the church—people like these Macedonians and Corinthians, and like us too—are not just those with some sort of taste for religious matters. No, the really important thing about these people is that they find themselves in a totally altered situation. If they really grasp their situation, they know that their whole lives have been reordered, reshaped into fellowship life with God and fellowship with one another. This life of fellowship means the end of self-possession. The people of the church are no longer their own. They do not own themselves. They have been set free from the curse of thinking that everything they are and everything they have can be treated as their own property. For they don't belong to themselves; they belong to Christ, and because they belong to him they also belong to one another. And belonging to Christ and to one another is not a matter of regret; it doesn't mean giving up life but finding life by being dispossessed.

Because all of this is true, the people of the church cannot but render practical assistance to those with whom God has set them in fellowship. They must serve them; they must share in the service of the saints. This service takes the form of sacrifice, of self-giving. These Macedonian Christians, Paul says, "gave themselves first to the Lord and then by the will of God to us" (2 Cor 8:5).

Grace, God's grace, evokes giving; it evokes service, the humble offering of aid to those in necessity or tribulation. To deny their fellows the help they need, to hold back, would be to contradict the gospel; it would be to act as if there were no fellowship, as if there were no abundant generosity of God, as if there were no miracle of grace out of which we all live. It would be to refuse to know something that we already do know—what Paul calls here, at the climax of the passage, "the grace of our Lord Jesus Christ" (2 Cor 8:9).

With this, we reach the very heart of the matter of generosity. "You know the grace of our Lord Jesus Christ, that though he was rich, yet for your sake he became poor, so that you by his poverty might become rich" (2 Cor 8:9). What is Paul doing here? Two things, I think. First, Paul is setting forth Jesus Christ himself as the example of generosity and self-giving. Jesus Christ, God in the flesh, emptied himself; he took upon himself human form, the form of a servant, and became obedient to death. Jesus' poverty is just this: his renunciation of protective self-possession; his unreserved fellowship with those in desperate straits; his turning to them; his utter concentration on their well-being; his giving of himself even to the point of death for the sake of their survival. He laid down his life for his friends. And, says Paul, we are to do the same.

But there's a second thing: Paul is saying that because Jesus Christ did all these things—because he lived in fellowship with us, and because he served us to the very end—then by his poverty we've become rich, rich beyond compare. We've come to share in the sheer, limitless abundance of God, with whom there are no half-measures but only unimaginable treasure beyond compare. And because we're rich, then we're set free for generosity. We're able to act in a way that echoes the grace of Jesus Christ himself. We don't replace that grace by something of our own; we don't even repeat it. We echo the grace of Jesus Christ; in our generosity is heard the faint reverberation of the one majestic act of generosity, God's own act of taking flesh, of taking up our hopeless cause, of redeeming us from poverty and darkness and death, and of sharing the treasures of his grace with us. Because he was these things and did these things, we have everything to give, and we have nothing to lose.

Such, in brief compass, is what Paul means by Christian generosity. It takes its rise in the grace of God. It's an overflow of abundance in the midst of affliction and poverty. It involves fellowship and service. And, above all, it's an echo of the grace of the Lord Jesus.

What must we do? Well, preachers in this cathedral, at least, don't usually know most of the congregation or their circumstances, and it's unwise and unhelpful to lay the law down too closely. But one thing that, with Paul, we can say: "see that you excel in this act of grace also" (2 Cor 8:7).

To do that—to excel in the gracious work of generosity—will involve different things for different people. For some of us it may mean learning to live with less material well-being and security than we would like. For others, it may involve a growth into joyful trust of God, which will emancipate us to become generous. For all of us, however, it will involve some sort of conversion, some changing of our hearts and wills, some shaping of us so that we become the people of Christ. Later in 2 Corinthians, Paul says this: "Whoever sows sparingly will also reap sparingly, and whoever sows bountifully will also reap bountifully. ... And God is able to make all grace abound to you, so that having all sufficiency in all things at all times, you may abound in every good work" (2 Cor 9:6, 8).

Let each of us examine ourselves. Amen.

XX

GENTLENESS

BROTHERS, if anyone is caught in any transgression, you who are spiritual should restore him in a spirit of gentleness. Keep watch on yourself, lest you too be tempted. Bear one another's burdens, and so fulfill the law of Christ. For if anyone thinks he is something, when he is nothing, he deceives himself.

GALATIANS 6:1–3

One of the hallmarks of the genuine Christian community is the way in which it deals with failure. More particularly: one of the tests of authentic Christian common life is whether we can find ways of facing and overcoming the sins and weaknesses that continue to burden the church.

Finding that kind of common life—finding a way of being together that does indeed face up to sin's reality but which is not crushed by it—involves a couple of things. It involves truthfulness. It involves getting beyond the pretense that we aren't sinners. It involves facing up to the fact that there is sin in the church and that the church can only flourish under God if we confess that fact. Part of the church's struggle to live out its calling is learning honesty, not hiding from judgment, and so being a place where sin is not glossed over or explained away but acknowledged and confessed. But alongside truthfulness is something else. There is gentleness; there is a peculiar Christian forbearance, a peculiarly

Christian way of dealing with the weaknesses of others, which expresses the character of the gospel and which fulfills the law of Christ.

As it governs its life by this twin requirement of truthfulness and gentleness, the church will express what it means to be a congregation under the gospel, an assembly of those whose lives have been transfigured by God's saving presence in Jesus Christ through the power of the Holy Spirit.

Let's think a bit about what's involved in the second of those two requirements, the requirement of gentleness. "If anyone is caught in any transgression, you who are spiritual should restore him in a spirit of gentleness" (Gal 6:1). Gentleness is not indifference to sin. It's not mere softness, pretending that sin isn't sin, because that's not a way of dealing with failure but a way of avoidance. Gentleness is truthful, realistic, looks failure in the eye and sees it for what it is. But it doesn't fall into the hostility that so often threatens to engulf us when we try to deal with the sins of others. Gentleness is the opposite of the fierce, bitter, censorious, accusatory attitude that very quickly mars the way in which we handle failure. It deals gently with failure, not because it underestimates or minimizes the seriousness of sin, but because gentleness is in accordance with the deep truth of the gospel.

Why is that so? Why is gentleness a requirement of the gospel of Christ? Paul gives us three reasons.

First, we are to deal gently with failure because the sinners of whom Paul is speaking here are those who have been *overtaken* in trespass. They are those who have fallen into a snare and got themselves in a mess. That doesn't mean that they are innocent, that they're victims and not perpetrators, but it does mean that they are not to be dealt with as if they were hard, deliberate dealers in vice. There are such hard people, of course, even in the church, and holiness demands that they be dealt with in a pretty determined way. But what Paul has in mind here is those who, through weakness or immaturity or foolishness, get themselves in a real tangle. And what they need is help, not just reproof. They need the kind of friendly assistance that each member of the fellowship is to offer to each other member; they need to be built up, not crushed; they need to be brought back into the company of the holy, not sent packing because they've done what the rest of us would probably end up doing in their place.

Second, we're to deal gently with failure because we must bear in mind our own weaknesses. "Keep watch on yourself," Paul tells the one who fancies himself as a bit of a hanging judge in the church and can't wait to lay into his neighbor who got into a muddle: "keep watch on yourself, lest you too be tempted" (Gal 6:1). Excessive severity in criticizing others usually goes hand in hand with a basic incapacity to see ourselves as we really are—a basic deficiency in admitting that we, too, are fallible and frail, that if we haven't sinned, it's usually only because we haven't had opportunity.

There's no room for pride, nor for the self-promoting holiness that isn't really holy at all but is very unholy self-reliance and self-satisfaction. "If anyone thinks he is something, when he is nothing, he deceives himself" (Gal 6:2). It's that self-deception Paul is exposing here. At the heart of the deception is a drastic miscalculation about the nature of the Christian life. The miscalculation consists in thinking that our holiness as Christians is something that we've achieved and that we possess. We fall into the trap of thinking that our moral performance is something on which we can congratulate ourselves, that we really are something, and so we think we have the right to use our achievement as a weapon against others. For Paul, that's a refusal of the real truth of the gospel, which is that in and of ourselves we're nothing—in other words, that everything we are and do is from Christ. And if everything is from Christ, if the Christian life is not achievement but gift, then contempt for others when they fall is fundamentally false. The gospel is about grace, and because it's about grace, it is about compassion.

Third, we're to deal gently with failure because we are to "bear one another's burdens, and so fulfill the law of Christ" (Gal 6:2).

Our companions in the church of Jesus Christ fail—they fall into error, they give in to weakness, they dishonor the gospel in some way. And because of this they are in need; they've hurt themselves, and more than anything they need our assistance. In them we hear once again an echo of the state of all humankind apart from the gospel. They're burdened; they're bruised and weakened by sin; they must hear once more a word that repeats to them the good news and speaks comfort and cleansing. And it is now our task, as their brothers and sisters, to speak that word—to say to them what the gospel says.

It isn't our task to refuse to say that word; it isn't our task to speak some word of condemnation other than that pronounced by the gospel. It is, very simply, our task to pronounce to them the word that takes away the burden of sin. And in so doing—in bearing their burdens, in freely and open-heartedly rendering them assistance and fellowship—we do something of infinite value. We *fulfill the law of Christ*. Paul doesn't mean we observe some rule; he means we fill out, we complete, the pattern for human life that is embodied in Jesus.

Here we have the very heart of the matter. Why are we not to be harsh and hostile? Why are we to be gentle? Because God in Christ acts thus in our regard. God himself, in the person of his Son, sees the entirety of human misery and failure, the hopelessness with which we thrash around in our sins. He does not pass us by but stops on his way and helps us. He makes pretty plain to us that we're in a mess and that we're in our mess because we're fools and sinners.

But as he shows us the truth, he succors us; with infinite mercy, condescension, and compassion he takes upon himself the burden of our sins—and not only carries it, but carries it away. We, of course, cannot do that for any other person; we cannot bear away a person's sins, for that is the work of God alone. And we need not bear another person's sins, because God has already done so. What we can do, however, is in speech and action say the one thing that must be said to our sinful companion in the church:

Christ has borne your sin. He has taken it away. And as we say that, not only in word but in deed, then we restore our companion to fellowship.

The aim of dealing with sin is not to publicize the faults of others; it's not to run some terrible, self-righteous campaign; it's not to make sure that we're known to be clean by showing how unclean everyone else is. The aim is reconciliation, the rebuilding of the life and fellowship of the church, and the restoration of our companions to the common life.

All this, Paul tells us, is what *you who are spiritual* ought to do. The spiritual, of course, aren't some sort of deluxe Christians; they're simply the baptized, those who have been given the Holy Spirit. Talking of the gift of the Spirit in this context is crucial, because it's very hard for us to imagine a church in which these practices of the bearing of burdens, of reconciliation and restoration, of gentleness, could really go on.

Is this just another bit of utopian dreaming? I think my answer is this: of course we can't imagine a Christian fellowship in which such things go on. It's impossible. But we aren't called to imagine it. We're called to ask for the gift of God's Spirit to make it so, to give us gentleness, to teach us the law of Christ, to help us bear one another's burdens.

Gentleness, Paul has told us in Galatians 5, is a fruit of the Spirit. And so it is for the Spirit that we must pray—that he would deign to enliven our fellowship; that he would teach us how to see our companions' need; that he would give us grace to assist those who have stumbled. "If we live by the Spirit, let us also keep in step with the Spirit" (Gal 5:25).

May God give us grace to learn these things, through Jesus Christ our Lord. Amen.

XXI

JUDGMENT

JUDGE not, that you be not judged. For with the judgment
you pronounce you will be judged, and with the measure
you use it will be measured to you. Why do you see the
speck that is in your brother's eye, but do not notice the
log that is in your own eye? Or how can you say to your
brother, "Let me take the speck out of your eye," when
there is the log in your own eye? You hypocrite, first take
the log out of your own eye, and then you will see clearly
to take the speck out of your brother's eye.

MATTHEW 7:1–5

One of the hallmarks of the genuine Christian community is
the way in which it deals with failure. More particularly: one
of the tests of authentic Christian common life is whether we can
find ways of facing and overcoming the sins and weaknesses that
continue to burden the church.

The church of Jesus Christ is to strive to be a place of transformed judgment. It's to try to be a place where the disorder that
afflicts the human activity of judging is overcome so that authentic
judgment can once again flourish. That means, very simply, that
the church is to be a place where people are engaged in the business of trying to see and speak the truth. Engaging in that business,
however, is no easy affair.

Seeing the truth, discriminating, isn't the straightforward business we often make it out to be. It's not a matter in which all that's

needed is a bit of common sense and a measure of determination. Seeing the truth always involves *coming* to see the truth, and we need to *come* to see the truth because for most of the time we live in half-truth or untruth—in a sort of shadowy realm in which judgment is just impossible. Seeing the truth and making judgments involves us being dragged out of the shadows and into the light, usually kicking and screaming. In short, the transformation of judgment is part of what's involved in that transformation of the entirety of human life that we call "regeneration," our being made new by the converting activity of God—Father, Son, and Spirit. And Jesus' words from Matthew—"Judge not"—invite us to reflect on what's involved in that transformation.

"Judge not." In these words, Jesus doesn't call us to abandon or suspend judgment; he calls us, rather, to renounce the diseased forms of judgment that have so infected our life together. The object of his attack, in other words, is not judgment itself but the perversion of judgment.

Judgment is a way in which we are related to the truth. To make a judgment and to speak in judgment is to perceive and articulate the truth. And it's because of this that judgment is so basic to human life: basic because truth is basic, and basic because the absence of truth is ruinous for human life and fellowship.

We see readily enough in public life how people engage in the bad business of ignoring, elaborating on, or trimming the truth to suit their own interests. You don't need to be a politician or a media baron to do that: there can be very few of us who haven't at one time or another seen how in the workplace or domestic circle truth gets lost in the shuffle when people cruise ahead to get what they want out of life. Closer to home, we know, if we have a modicum of self-knowledge, that one of the things that ruins our personal lives is our amazing capacity to hide from or gloss over the truth. Publicly and privately, truth is crucial to human flourishing, for if once we cease to see what really is the case, then we cannot act truthfully—we cannot be truthful human beings. It's for just this reason that judgment is an essential activity in the church of Jesus Christ, for if the church is a place where we're learning how to be human, then one of the first lessons must be how to see reality without illusion or evasion and to begin to judge.

We often fail to see this about the church, often think and act as if the church were a place where we're supposed to self-consciously *avoid* judgment. Sometimes, sadly, we turn away from the necessity of judgment on simple laissez-faire principles in which the only norm of judgment is private conscience—absolute, inviolable, and never subject to the judgment of others. But all we end up doing is making the church a shapeless sack of arbitrary opinions; we make the church into something that is almost infinitely elastic, which will stretch to fit any shape of person, any way of life. All that does is say that what we are, what we think, and what we do just doesn't matter.

At other times, we flee from judgment because we assume that all judging is necessarily perverse. That is, we may fear that judging is inherently a matter of adopting a harsh, unforgiving, superior, or condemnatory attitude to others. "Who are we to judge?" we ask, with a sigh. The problem here, however, is not skepticism but a kind of misdirected humility in which—faced with the way we often abuse the activity of judging—we give up on the possibility of ever reaching and uttering a true judgment.

But abandoning the possibility of judgment is ruinous. (That, of course, is the point of the story of Jethro urging Moses to set up a system of small-claims magistrates in Israel: God's people need an orderly means of keeping truth before their eyes [Exod 18:13–23]). When judgment goes, truth goes; and when truth goes out of the church, the church will have very little with which to edify itself or to encourage, console, and chasten the wider society.

Nevertheless—and it's a big nevertheless—there's a perversion of judgment that Jesus condemns. The essence of the perversity is this: *judgment can become a means of wicked self-interest.* How does this take place?

Consider what judgment ought properly to be about. Real, authentic human judgment is an attempt to repeat the judgment of God. It's an attempt to point to, to indicate, the judgment of God, who is himself the truth and who makes the truth known to us. An authentic human judgment isn't a mere point of view or opinion, something that I as judge have created out of my own resources; the making of judgments in the church is by no means a matter of forcing the opinions of some on to the consciences of others. Proper judgment comes from seeing the truth and saying what we see. It's an act of witness: it bears testimony to the truth, it says what we *must* say if we are to live in the truth.

Perverted judgment is a very different animal. It's not a matter of humble testimony to the truth of God, of repeating the truth that we have been told, but a means of self-exaltation. Perverse judgment is a servant of one master and one master alone: my self-interest. In this way, perverse judgment is in league with a disorderly and utterly destructive desire that is never far from the surface in every human being—the desire to exalt myself above my fellows. It's an attempt to exalt myself by being not only more powerful, attractive, or confident than others but also more righteous, more holy, more acceptable to God.

We don't need to inspect ourselves for more than a second to see this at work in our day-to-day commerce with our neighbors. Who doesn't enjoy being the sharpest or wittiest critic in our social circle, even if the cost is the reputation or honor of another? Which of us has never felt that eagerness to probe around in the misdeeds of others in the hope of finding something juicy? Who among us is a stranger to that delight we feel in retelling to others some sin or failure on the part of one of our neighbors—some slight fault, perhaps, but one that we can make out to be a crime and rejoice in doing so?

Why is it that we take such inordinate pleasure in these things? In the end, it's because making these kinds of false judgments serves a very sinister purpose: it helps us maintain the comforting but deadly illusion that we aren't really sinners. Once sin can be seen as something in *others*, then I can let myself off the hook. I may go wrong here and there, I may waver, I may slip, but at heart I am safe and sanctified because I'm not like these others. And it's against these others that my judgment is directed as a weapon—an urbane and intelligent weapon with all the appearance of holiness but which is in fact a very nasty and destructive instrument indeed.

False or perverted judgment destroys two things. First, *it destroys my neighbor's reputation*. It's a lie, and lies eat away at community. No society, church, or family can survive a regime in which falsehood is allowed to reign. But *it also destroys me*, the false judge. It breaks my submission to the truth and means that I become blind. I think I see, because I believe the lies I tell myself; I believe my neighbor is a greater sinner than I am, I believe that I'm purer and more trustworthy than others. But in fact I'm just a hypocrite—I'm play-acting, pretending to see what I cannot see because of the log in my own eye (Matt 7:3). And so my judgment destroys me also.

Such is the sad state of truthful judgment among us. How may our judging be healed? How may it be rescued from its allegiance to sin and self-interest and returned to the hands of godliness and obedience?

Once again: we don't get anywhere by letting the church community, or ourselves, drift into an indiscriminate, indifferent attitude. Indifference isn't humility or charity; it's a pretext or occasion for sin. We are *obligated* to judge, because we're the kind of creatures to whom it matters what really is the case about the world. But if we're obligated to judge, we're obligated to judge in the right way. And the right way would be something like this.

True judgment is an indication of or witness to God's judgment, God's truth. Such a witness properly involves two things. First, *it's most properly directed against ourselves, and only by extension is it directed to others*. "With the judgment you pronounce you will be judged, and with the measure you use it will be measured to you" (Matt 7:2). We stand under the same truth which we invoke when we judge our neighbor. If we don't see this, we aren't really judging: all we're doing is pretending to judge.

We will only judge truthfully, therefore, if we know that we are ourselves judged by God, who alone is competent to declare the truth. There is all the difference in the world between that self-assured destroyer of the reputations of others and the person who only dares to judge because he or she has first of all been broken by God's judgment. Judgment begins in silence, and it begins in hearing the word spoken by God against us.

Second, *true judgment that witnesses to God's judgment will be undertaken in fear and trembling*. It will be a very far cry indeed from that corrupt enjoyment we take in running down others. It will be self-mistrustful, because it knows how hard it is for us to accept the truth and that it is harder still to speak it clearly and with charity. It knows the dangers of judgment; it knows the pleasures we take in having power over our neighbors; it knows how much we love to be safe from the truth. The true judge will, therefore, be fearful: however inescapable the obligation to judge may be, the true judge will always tremble at its prospect.

In the early 1720s, Joseph Butler, later to become bishop of Bristol and then Durham, was preacher in the Rolls Chapel in London, and his sermons have become classics of acute moral psychology. In one of the sermons, he remarks:

> There is ... in the generality of mankind, an absence of doubt or distrust ... as to their moral character and behaviour; and likewise a disposition to take for granted that all is right and well with them in these respects.

The root of this, he says, is twofold: a failure to exercise judgment upon ourselves, and an inflamed self-love, a steady eye to our own interest. He's right: the hardest thing in the world is to see clearly, and the biggest obstacle to seeing clearly is our unshakeable belief that we *can* see clearly.

How may we get beyond such conceit and prejudice in our own favor and so come to make truthful judgments? The simple answer is: we can't. No amount of practice or self-cultivation will help us see and judge truthfully. And so judgment begins not in assurance but in prayer. Most of all, it begins in prayer for the coming of the Spirit of God. For it's the office of the Spirit to lead us into truth; it's therefore through the Spirit that we may discern and speak the truth. And that's why—with fear and trembling, expectant, ready to hear—we pray with Thomas Cranmer:

> Heavenly Father, at whose hand the weak shall suffer no wrong nor the mighty escape just judgment; pour thy grace upon thy servants ... that by their true, faithful, and diligent execution of judgment ... thou mayest be glorified, the commonwealth daily promoted and increased, and we all live in peace and quietness, godliness and virtue; through Jesus Christ our Lord. Amen.

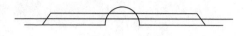

PART V

PROCLAIMING SALVATION

XXII

PROPHETIC SPEECH

"BUT say to them, The days are near, and the fulfillment of every vision. For there shall be no more any false vision or flattering divination within the house of Israel. For I am the LORD; I will speak the word that I will speak, and it will be performed. It will no longer be delayed, but in your days, O rebellious house, I will speak the word and perform it, declares the Lord GOD."

And the word of the LORD came to me: "Son of man, behold, they of the house of Israel say, 'The vision that he sees is for many days from now, and he prophesies of times far off.' Therefore say to them, Thus says the Lord GOD: None of my words will be delayed any longer, but the word that I speak will be performed, declares the Lord GOD."

The word of the LORD came to me: "Son of man, prophesy against the prophets of Israel, who are prophesying, and say to those who prophesy from their own hearts: 'Hear the word of the LORD!' Thus says the Lord GOD, Woe to the foolish prophets who follow their own spirit, and have seen nothing! Your prophets have been like jackals among ruins, O Israel. You have not gone up into the breaches, or built up a wall for the house of Israel, that it might stand in battle in the day of the LORD. They have seen false visions and lying divinations. They say, 'Declares the LORD,' when the LORD has not sent them, and yet they expect him to fulfill their word. Have you not seen a false vision and uttered a lying divination, whenever you have said, 'Declares the LORD,' although I have not spoken?"

Therefore thus says the Lord GOD: "Because you have uttered falsehood and seen lying visions, therefore behold, I am against you, declares the Lord GOD. My hand will be against the prophets who see false visions and who give lying divinations. They shall not be in the council of my people, nor be enrolled in the register of the house of Israel, nor shall they enter the land of Israel. And you shall know that I am the Lord GOD.

EZEKIEL 12:23–13:9

"May the Lord grant that we might meditate upon the heavenly mysteries of wisdom and progress in true piety, to his glory and our edification. Amen" (John Calvin).

As we turn to a hard passage from Ezekiel, we look at the speech of the people of God from the angle of "speech as *prophecy*." What, we may ask, does it mean for the people of God to be a community in which prophetic speech happens, in which prophecy is spoken and heard as God's word?

We sometimes think of prophecy as if it were a sort of long-range historical radar—a means of foretelling the future, even some kind of collective horoscope, giving us advance warning of what to avoid and what to look forward to. But in biblical terms, prophecy isn't simply predictive, foretelling the future; primarily, it's about declaring the will, purpose, and character of God. First and foremost, prophecy declares who God is and what God's purposes for his people are. The prophet is one who interprets the life of God's people by setting that life in the light of God's revealed nature and command. And so prophecy does a lot more than predict: it indicates who God is; it testifies to God's activity in the world and among his people; it announces the command of God. In short: prophecy is the way in which the people of God are brought up short by the claim of truth.

Prophecy like this isn't just natural human speech. Of course, it's human words, spoken by an all-too-fallible human speaker. Yet even as such, prophecy is from God, in a very real sense God's own speech. "Thus says the Lord God," the prophet says—and those words aren't just a bit of added earnestness, a way of grabbing attention or arrogating authority, but something essential to the nature of prophetic speech. It's that speaking which is to be traced to God; in it, through it, God communicates. Here in prophetic speech, as Ezekiel has it: "For I am the LORD; I will speak the word that I will speak" (Ezek 12:25). And because prophecy is in the ultimate sense *God's* speaking, it's judgment.

It interrupts; it intercepts the steady jog of human life; it overturns; it breaks into a situation that doesn't want to be spoken to in such a way, which would prefer to remain unaddressed, self-enclosed, quietly getting on with its own business. Prophecy means crisis, and, therefore, it means struggle. Prophecy is one of the focal points of the continual struggle between God and humanity: between God, who seeks to speak the word of truth, and us humans, who would rather be left to ourselves. Wherever there is prophecy, there is deafness, that closing off of human life that resists the speaking of God.

It's this struggle that is the theme of the passage from Ezekiel before us. It sets before us two aspects of this clash between God and the people of God that prophecy always evokes, two ways in which God's people seek to keep God at a quiet distance so that they may rest in peace. First, prophecy can be greeted with cynicism. This is what Ezekiel faces: run of the mill, commonplace cynical disbelief that prophecy is really speech from God. Nothing comes of it, Ezekiel's countrymen tell him, so it looks as if the whole thing is just empty. God's word doesn't happen; God doesn't speak; and to expect that God will speak is at best quaint and at worst a bit of obsolete religious ballast we need to throw overboard.

Nowadays we sometimes use a more elevated term for this kind of cynicism: we call it "secularization." But it comes down to the same thing: it means treating human life and history as if there were no action or speech of God to contend with. It even means treating the life and history of the people of God in the same way—as if we were to expect no action or speech of God, as if our life were for all intents and purposes secular, as if the project of the church were just that—a human project in which we can expect no intervening word from God.

We will fail to hear what Ezekiel has to say unless we realize what it is that's so attractive about that cynical disbelief in prophecy. It's powerfully attractive, because it means God can be kept at a safe distance. "Son of man, behold, they of the house of Israel say, 'The vision that he sees is for many days from now, and he prophesies of times far off'" (Ezek 12:27). The silence of prophecy means the people of God can breathe a huge sigh of relief: no more interruption; no more challenge; no more responsibility to this alien, intrusive voice of God. We can, finally, be left to our own devices and get on with life in the way we think best. Here, perhaps, is the great temptation for all forms of institutional religion: the replacing of lively openness with being addressed by a worldly-wise but in the end callous and deadly inattentiveness to the speech of God.

As God's prophetic word comes to the people of God, then, it can encounter cynicism. But it can also encounter another form of resistance, which is falsehood. Here God's prophetic speaking among us isn't rejected but replaced. It isn't silenced, but a substitute is put in its place, so that its power to contradict, judge, and challenge is muffled. "Woe to the foolish prophets who follow their own spirit, and have seen nothing! … They have seen false visions and lying divinations. They say, 'Declares the LORD,' when the LORD has not sent them, and yet they expect him to fulfill their word" (Ezek 13:3, 6). This is a so-called word of God that isn't the word of God; it isn't from God but self-originating; it doesn't stem from vision (from that seeing of God's truth, which God alone grants) but from invention. And so it's falsehood—it isn't something that God appoints to be said but merely something imagined or created, what Ezekiel calls a delusive vision.

Of course, this may not be a matter of deliberate falsification in the life of the people of God. It may be a word that is spoken and received in good faith. More often than not, it's the product of an honest sense that we're left to our own resources in the church, that if a word is to be spoken, we have to speak it because God doesn't speak, and so we're left to exercise our best powers of judgment. Great tracts of contemporary church life are based on such principles. In practical terms, we don't expect that God should speak to us, and so we have to search our minds and speak to ourselves. When that happens, we become very deferential to other voices, especially those which present themselves as experts in one or another field of human affairs, and we can often land ourselves in a political process in the church in which we're so scrupulous about listening to every possible voice that we fail to attend to the one word that is, in fact, spoken to us—namely, the prophetic voice of God.

It's quite possible for the church to drift into a way of life that—for all its spirituality, for all its honest searching of conscience, self-questioning, and teachableness—in effect has given up listening to God. The church can cease to be a church of the word, usually, of course, without even realizing it. And the terrible price which is paid is the loss of truth, and so alienation from God himself. "Therefore thus says the Lord GOD: 'Because you have uttered falsehood and seen lying visions, therefore behold, I am against you, declares the Lord GOD. My hand will be against the prophets who see false visions and who give lying divinations. They shall not be in the council of my people, nor be enrolled in the register of the house of Israel, nor shall they enter the land of Israel. And you shall know that I am the Lord GOD'" (Ezek 13:8–9).

I suspect most of us are inclined to smile indulgently at such words: it sounds like the rhetoric of a world that has gone forever.

But it's deadly serious. The people of God, the church, isn't constituted in such a way that it speaks its own word to itself or must make up its own mind. It's constituted as a place where God's speech is listened to with earnestness, astonishment, penitence, and joy. If in pride the church decides it prefers its own word, or if in despair the church decides that it has only its own word, then it becomes just a broken wall, a ruin, not a temple, and there can be no peace in its midst.

"For I am the LORD; I will speak the word that I will speak, and it will be performed. It will no longer be delayed, but in your days, O rebellious house, I will speak the word and perform it, declares the Lord GOD" (Ezek 12:25). Ezekiel doesn't argue with cynicism or falsehood; he doesn't seek by argument to persuade that, after all, there are good grounds for believing that God will speak. He simply declares. And he declares because he's a prophet and knows that the obstacle to hearing prophecy isn't in the reason but in the will. If the church is to be a place where prophecy is heard, then we need to become different people, people who have been converted into hearers. This is no once-for-all event; it's a permanent process in the church, which is always threatened by refusal to listen to God and which therefore always needs to exercise diligence in rooting out of itself that stubbornness which will not be spoken to. What does this involve? What needs to happen in the life of the church if this part of its life is to be kept alive? Two things might be mentioned.

First, we need to learn repentance. Repentance isn't an occasional motif in the life of the Christian church but one of its most basic activities. Additionally, repentance isn't to be limited to the moral sphere, as if all that we need to repent of is our ethical failure. Of course, repentance is needed there, but equally, we need to learn repentance in the sphere of the church's apprehension of the truth. We don't just act wrongly; we also fail in our attention to the truth, and so we need repentance in this sphere, too. Indeed, repentance is fundamental to learning, and a church that does not seek to learn, which isn't constantly being dragged around to face the truth, can hardly be described as a church at all. True repentance is, of course, not neurotic self-accusation, beating ourselves on the breasts and entertaining all sorts of dire thoughts about ourselves. *Repentance is simply consent to the truth of God's judgment.* Thereby it's a movement away from falsehood, away from the silencing of the word of God into a real attention, a fresh and obedient hearing of prophecy in our midst. Such hearing isn't a natural skill, and it can't be cultivated by natural means. It's the Spirit's gift, and so a church that seeks to be repentant in its attention to God must be a church in which prayer for the Spirit's coming is paramount.

Second, we need to recover a proper confidence in the reality that God is communicative. If Scripture is to be taken seriously, God isn't mute; God isn't distant and silent, moodily closed up in himself and keeping his own counsel. In the Son and the Spirit he's outgoing, and in his prophetic word he speaks. More than anything else we need to learn how to be expectant of God's speaking, how to be communities of people who are vivid, alert, and hopeful, because God is a speaking God.

Much is involved here: a lightness of institutional structure so that God's word doesn't get buried beneath protocol; a recovery of confident use of Scripture as the present place where the prophetic word can be heard; a discernment in listening to the voices of those outside the church; but above all, again, prayerfulness, in which we wait upon the speaking of God.

At the end of his life, the great reformer John Calvin lectured on the prophet Ezekiel, and by the time he got to the end of chapter twelve he was mortally sick, unable to leave his house and dictating his thoughts from his bed. The prayer with which we began this sermon was Calvin's customary prayer at the opening of all his lectures, and it maybe fitting to close with a prayer he used at the end of lecturing on Ezekiel 12:

Almighty God, since in real measure you spare us, and meantime warn us with unmistakable signs of your wrath, grant us in good time to repent, lest negligence possess our minds and hearts and also dissipate our judgment. May we be attentive ... to your Word, and may we be so zealous to reconcile ourselves to you that for the future, having been reborn of your Spirit, we may ever glorify your name in Jesus Christ our Lord.

Amen.

XXIII

ABANDONED TO GOD'S CAUSE

O Lord, you have deceived me,
   and I was deceived;
you are stronger than I,
   and you have prevailed.
I have become a laughingstock all the day;
   everyone mocks me.
For whenever I speak, I cry out,
   I shout, "Violence and destruction!"
For the word of the Lord has become for me
   a reproach and derision all day long.
If I say, "I will not mention him,
   or speak any more in his name,"
there is in my heart as it were a burning fire
   shut up in my bones,
and I am weary with holding it in,
   and I cannot.
For I hear many whispering.
   Terror is on every side!
"Denounce him! Let us denounce him!"
   say all my close friends,
   watching for my fall.
"Perhaps he will be deceived;
   then we can overcome him
   and take our revenge on him."

But the Lord is with me as a dread warrior;
> therefore my persecutors will stumble;
> they will not overcome me.

They will be greatly shamed,
> for they will not succeed.

Their eternal dishonor
> will never be forgotten.

O Lord of hosts, who tests the righteous,
> who sees the heart and the mind,

let me see your vengeance upon them,
> for to you have I committed my cause.

JEREMIAH 20:7–12

It is the consistent witness of Scripture that to be a prophet or an apostle is to face affliction. It's not the lot of the prophet or the apostle to win a ready hearing, to be acclaimed and honored. Quite the opposite: to speak for God as prophet or apostle is to suffer for the word. The word isn't the prophet's glory but his reproach and a matter of derision.

Why is this? Why does testifying to the word of God afflict the prophet? The answer, I think, is this: prophecy is trapped between God and falsehood. Prophecy—human speaking of God's word—gets crushed between the God who speaks and the rebellious hearer. For it's the office of the prophet to speak the truth of God. The prophet, like also the apostle, is commissioned by God to be a mouthpiece of God's own speaking; the prophet's voice is that human instrument through which God addresses the people of God in judgment and promise. It's this speaking of the truth that's at the heart of the prophet's affliction.

He *suffers* for the word of God; because the truth of God must be spoken and must be spoken by him, he is afflicted. What afflicts the prophet, therefore, isn't just particularly difficult circumstances or a grim personality. The root of the affliction is that speaking the word of God, speaking the truth, is always done in the face of human resistance to the truth. The prophet or the apostle isn't a popular entertainer or even some sort of upmarket preacher who can send a frisson of religious excitement coursing through our psyches. No! Once again, it's the office of the prophet to speak the truth of God, and therefore—because God's truth judges and hurts and exposes its hearers—to suffer for the word.

In what does the suffering consist? Prophetic affliction consists, in part, in a sense that the prophet's calling—that to which God has summoned the prophet and which is the chief business of the prophet's life—is inescapable. He's in the hands of God, and there is no release. "If I say, 'I will not mention him, or speak any more in his name,' there is in my heart as it were a burning fire shut up in my bones, and I am weary with holding it in, and I cannot" (Jer 20:9). Jeremiah almost feels the divine calling and appointment as a curse, as an iron necessity laid on him; it's certainly not cheerful and free and fulfilling. But, even more than this, for Jeremiah prophetic affliction consists in simple human rejection. This is a point of some importance, because it takes us closer to the heart of what the institution of prophecy is all about.

Properly understood, prophecy is an act of charity. It's not just unfocused, purposeless condemnation—not just the prophet laying about him and knocking over whatever gets in his way. Prophecy is speaking the word of God for the sake of others, bearing witness to God's truth because hearing and living by the truth is the only foundation for human fellowship and human flourishing. The prophet isn't to be thought of as some religious lone ranger figure, apart from the common life of the people of God, shouting abuse from the touchline.

The prophet's aim is the welfare of the city of God's people. Far from being antisocial, his office is concerned with the building up of the common life of God's people by setting it in the light of the truth. Yet the affliction of the prophet is that it's precisely these bonds of common life that are denied him. Because he speaks the truth, and because the truth is always resisted, he is denied the fellowship he seeks to build. "I have become a laughingstock all the day; everyone mocks me. … For I hear many whispering. Terror is on every side! 'Denounce him! Let us denounce him!' say all my close friends, watching for my fall. 'Perhaps he will be deceived; then we can overcome him and take our revenge on him' " (Jer 20:7, 10). If prophecy is an act of charity, a work that seeks to edify by announcing the truth, it's nevertheless the fate of the prophet to discover that speaking the truth means rejection.

What answer is there to the prophet's affliction? There's immediately one very tempting solution to the dilemma, and it's in the figure of Pashur the priest, the chief officer in the house of the Lord, a man of some considerable religious and political clout (Jer 20:1). Pashur, we read, heard Jeremiah's prophecy and, realizing soon enough what it was about, had him hauled in, roughed up, and put in the cells for a night. All, of course, to no avail: as soon as he's out of the slammer, Jeremiah rounds on him (Jer 20:2–3). Pashur is a false prophet, says Jeremiah; that is, he does not seeks to rule the life of Israel by submitting it to the truth of God's word but by submitting it to much more tangible and apparently effective instruments of government, the exercise of power backed up by the use of force. And he will die, as he has lived, without the blessing of God.

We would be quite wrong, I think, to assume that Pashur is a thoroughly wicked man, obviously corrupt, obviously hostile to God. He may be, but he may also be nothing more terrible than a practical religious man of affairs, even in his own way a diligent leader of Israel. He's a man aware of the dangers of extremism, perhaps a man who thinks it's better to secure a little progress than to attempt everything and risk losing everything. But he's a false prophet because his relation to the truth is disturbed and because he has governed Israel in such a way that that disturbance has crept into the public life of God's people. He's a false prophet because he *calculates*; he calculates not just how to save his own skin or how to avoid the afflictions of the truth-speaking prophet, but also how to secure modest but real improvements. The false prophet is a realist; he knows that things may well move ahead if we're accommodating and mollifying, and if we steer clear of those terrible dark negatives that are Jeremiah's stock in trade.

All of this may be rather tempting to Jeremiah, affirming his desire to address the people of God and direct them in the way they should go while easing him of the afflictions of speaking the word of God without compromise. But—and for Jeremiah it's an all-important "but"—false prophecy isn't one form of prophecy. It isn't prophecy at all. The institution of prophecy cannot be tamed in this way. Limited or contained prophecy, prophecy held in check by some human boundaries, isn't from God. True prophetic speech—speech that addresses the people of God in God's name with God's word—is by its very nature disturbing, invasive, subversive. It can't become the servant of a human program, even a program of reform. It can't be muffled by routine, even if the routine is the prudent, steady progress of apparent godliness. However accommodating, however urbane, however dignified, false prophecy is resistance to truth and so resistance to judgment. That's why Jeremiah can't fulfill his office by making peace with the chief officer in the house of the Lord.

So what is left to Jeremiah? What answer is there to his affliction? His answer—if we can bear to hear it—is this: "But the LORD is with me as a dread warrior; therefore my persecutors will stumble; they will not overcome me. They will be greatly shamed, for they will not succeed. Their eternal dishonor will never be forgotten. O LORD of hosts, who tests the righteous, who sees the heart and the mind, let me see your vengeance upon them, for to you have I committed my cause" (Jer 20:11–12). It sounds, of course, unbelievably arrogant: God will pay you back; you'll see that I was right all along; God will humiliate you as you now humiliate me.

No doubt like the rest of us Jeremiah was tempted to use God in that way, as the sort of ultimate threat, the card to trump all other cards in a bid for power. But the real point of what he has to say lies elsewhere. And it's this: "to you have I committed my cause" (Jer 20:12). The point is not that God just underwrites Jeremiah's cause, as it were, and promises to provide ultimate sanctions whenever Jeremiah feels the need for them. Quite the opposite: the cause is not Jeremiah's, but God's. Jeremiah has renounced all attempts to look after himself, whether by making his peace with the authorities like Pashur or even by invoking God to wreak terminal destruction on his enemies. He has abandoned his cause entirely; he has put everything into the cause of God. So what matters isn't, in a real sense, Jeremiah's vindication but the vindication of God.

God is with Jeremiah as a dread warrior. But that does not mean that Jeremiah can outgun the opposition; it means that God himself will look after his own cause with his people. If Jeremiah himself will be vindicated and his afflictions put to an end, it will be only because God himself will act, and, above all, because God will himself establish the truth. God sees the heart and mind. God himself will speak and act to confirm Jeremiah's prophecy; God himself will take matters into his own hands.

So much for Jeremiah. What of us who hear this word now in the testimony of Scripture?

First, it is, I believe, proper for us to think of the Christian church as a whole as a prophetic community. The church is that human society in which, more than anything else, truth is spoken. The church of Jesus Christ is not a voluntary association of like-minded religious or moral devotees; what holds it together is not shared taste in matters of the mind or the heart or the spirit. The church is a prophetic community, an improbable collection of all kinds of people who assemble around the single fact that God speaks the truth in the gospel. Put another way: the church is prophetic because it is apostolic; it's the community that is drawn into being and kept in life because the apostles, like the prophets, bear witness to God's great interruptive act of speaking the truth in Jesus Christ through the power of the Holy Spirit.

The church is a prophetic and apostolic community in two orientations or trajectories. It is prophetic, first, in an *internal orientation* as it subjects itself to the word of God. The church lives on the basis of the prophetic word in that it lives under the tutelage of revelation. Because it is a prophetic community, the church does not seek to address itself with its own word; rather, it lives its life properly and authentically when it is regularly shaken by the word, overthrown by the word's promises and commands, docile to the word's presence.

Second, the church is prophetic in an *external orientation* because it bears witness to the world of the word that God speaks. Far from being turned in on itself, the church is commissioned to be a community that speaks: because it has heard, it bears witness; because it is prophetic, it is apostolic, sent to speak, to be a community of declaration. Turned to the word by the sheer power and authority of God, the church is simultaneously turned toward humanity in friendship and fellowship, saying the one thing that it can say, which is God's word of judgment and promise.

But this life in the word is always threatened; the church is—as Jeremiah shows with such vividness—always besieged by rejection. Sometimes it's threatened by overt hostility and contempt; more often, by polite disdain or by that sympathetic absorption of prophecy, that deadly spiritual cushioning of God so that we get religion without tears and without terror. If that's true, then at least one of the signs of the church's health will be suffering for the word. One of the marks of Christian authenticity is true affliction—not the false affliction of self-produced and self-righteous misery but the true affliction of refusing to shut up God's word within our bones.

But if all this is true—if the apostolic church is necessarily prophetic and necessarily afflicted by its prophetic calling and task—then there is a question here that we cannot escape: Why is this strange to us? Why do we often find it hard to envisage our church life in these terms? Most of all, I think it is because, like many mainline churches, Anglicans find themselves at the tail end of a tradition in which the Christian community and the civil community have been largely coextensive. Part of the legacy of that tradition is the idea that the church exists as a sort of moral influence on the body politic, a benevolent and increasingly indulgent conscience that pervades social reality but rarely gets caught up in much conflict.

The question that hangs over that whole pattern of church life is this: Can we sustain ourselves as a prophetic community when we allow ourselves to be cast in the role of proving the "values" to soften the impact of technocracy or the apparently benign forms of late capitalism that are riding a coach and horses through the common life of the nation?

In the end, I do not think we can continue to be a prophetic community unless we say a firm, "No," at this point. But we can only say, "No," when we have resolved to repent: to repent of our inattentiveness, of our resistance to the word, and of our refusal to be governed by the testimony in which God bears witness to himself. The only way to be a community of the word is to be a community of the word, and what we do today, as every day when we gather to worship, is just part of that steady endeavor to submit to truth, and therefore to be healed from falsehood and set free to speak the truth. Amen.

XXIV

CREATURES OF GRACE

I MYSELF am satisfied about you, my brothers, that you
yourselves are full of goodness, filled with all knowledge
and able to instruct one another. But on some points I have
written to you very boldly by way of reminder, because of
the grace given me by God to be a minister of Christ Jesus
to the Gentiles in the priestly service of the gospel of God,
so that the offering of the Gentiles may be acceptable, sanctified by the Holy Spirit. In Christ Jesus, then, I have reason
to be proud of my work for God. For I will not venture to
speak of anything except what Christ has accomplished
through me to bring the Gentiles to obedience—by word
and deed, by the power of signs and wonders, by the power
of the Spirit of God—so that from Jerusalem and all the
way around to Illyricum I have fulfilled the ministry of the
gospel of Christ; and thus I make it my ambition to preach
the gospel, not where Christ has already been named, lest
I build on someone else's foundation, but as it is written,

"Those who have never been told of him will see,
    and those who have never heard will understand."

ROMANS 15:14–21

The affliction of the prophet is that he simply cannot evade the
call of God to declare God's word. In the midst of untruth, in

the midst of rebellion against God's declaration of reality, it's the office of the prophet to be the herald of God's truth. The prophet is afflicted because he's caught between God and sin; speak he must, but in speaking he's almost crushed between the weight of his commission and the almost equal weight of its rejection. If the prophet survives, it's only because his affliction is overcome in the vindication of God. The prophet comes through his affliction, not because he stands up for his own cause, but because God will see to it that his word is shown for what it is: the true Word.

To be the church of Jesus Christ is to be a prophetic community, and therefore it's to share in both the prophet's affliction and the prophet's vindication. But the prophetic church is also the apostolic church; it stands in line not only with prophets like Jeremiah but also with apostles like Paul. And it's to Paul's reflections on his apostolic ministry in Romans 15 that we now turn in continuation of our study. What, we may ask, is the nature of Paul's apostolic ministry? How may what he has to say help us understand the apostolic commission of the whole church of Jesus Christ?

It's worth saying at the outset that apostolicity in ministry is something that is to be attributed to the whole church of Jesus Christ. Being an apostolic church is not, to nail the point, solely or even primarily about having bishops; more than anything, it's about being baptized. Apostolic ministry isn't the preserve of an order within the whole; the church of Jesus Christ in its entirety is apostolic. We (by which I mean Anglicans—visitors from other branches of the Christian family will have to forgive a bit of in-house polemic) have sometimes fallen into a rather bad habit of identifying apostolic ministry with the ministry of bishops and have thought that the church is apostolic because it is episcopal. Whatever else we may say about bishops, the office of bishop isn't an embodiment or guarantee or even, as ecumenists these days say, a sign of the apostolic character of Christ's church.

To say that the community of Jesus is apostolic is to say two things: that the church is faithful to the apostles' teaching, and that the church continues in the apostles' mission of proclaiming the gospel. It may be that a ministry of oversight is a necessary official testimony to the gospel; I believe it is necessary. But office and apostolicity aren't the same sort of thing. The gospel can never condense into order; order, office are witnesses, indicators of the reality of the gospel and the presence and activity of the risen Jesus. What keeps the church in being isn't the indicators but that which they indicate: Jesus Christ himself, the Lord of the church, in whose hands alone lie its past, its present, and its future.

Now, I begin there not just so we can get that issue off our collective chests but because it's something along these lines that Paul, the apostle of Jesus Christ, is talking about when he speaks of his own ministry. "I have written to you very boldly," he tells his readers (Rom 15:15). But his boldness is apostolic boldness— that is, it's something to which he's commissioned, something given to him. Whatever personal authority and charisma Paul may have had, whatever force his exhortation and example may have been able to exhort, doesn't matter in the end; what matters is an authority, a boldness, not his own but derived. What that apostolic authority and boldness derive from is his calling by Jesus Christ—something that he calls here the grace given to him to be a minister of Jesus Christ.

There are three matters here which call for our attention. The first concerns the origin of Paul's apostolic ministry. As an apostle, Paul isn't a self-made man. He's one called or appointed, and one sent by Christ. A self-appointed apostle isn't an apostle at all but an enemy of the gospel in just the same way that a prophet who takes upon himself the prophetic task cannot speak the truth of God but will always prophesy falsely. "How are they to preach unless they are sent?" Paul asks in Romans 10:15. Being an apostle is about precisely that: being called and sent, being arrested by Jesus Christ, gathered to him and drawn into the sphere of his lordship by his mercy, and then being impelled outward to speak in his name.

Being an apostle is a matter of divine appointment and sending. It's not a work of nature; it's not a matter of extending or refining natural capacities. Any such ideas would just reverse the direction of the apostle's ministry, which isn't from himself to others but from Jesus Christ himself and hence and only hence to the world. If the apostle is sent as a herald of grace, it's only because he is himself a creature of grace. The ministry of the apostle isn't a matter of the apostle's choice or even of some kind of inner compulsion. His commission rests solely on the name of the one by whom he is sent; in that name alone is his origin and authorization.

Immediately, of course, this has things to say to us about the apostolic character of the church—that is, about the apostolic character of the one, holy, and catholic church of which we find ourselves part. To be a community of Jesus Christ is to be apostolic, and to be apostolic is to be a creature of the gospel of grace. And to be a creature of grace is to be a community that bears the marks of that grace—a community, that is, not brought into being by decisions that we have made or commitments and convictions of our own devising. It's to be a sent community, a community assembled, overwhelmed, and appointed by an act and a voice that is not our own.

Can we—let us ask—bring ourselves to see how crucial this is for us? Churches like ours, which have acquired a measure of social stability and cultural solidity and even a bit of prestige, are always tempted to naturalize their lives—to think of their lives as an expression of our religious and moral natures. Such thoughts imperil the gospel; they drastically alter the character of the apostolic church. What creates the one church isn't us but the Holy Spirit of the one Lord Jesus Christ. What makes the church holy isn't human decision but election and baptism. What makes the church apostolic is God, so that, as Paul puts it, we *are* "because of the grace given [us]" (Rom 15:15).

If Paul's apostolic ministry thus has its origin in the grace of God, then, second, the agent of his ministry is, in the last resort, not Paul himself but Jesus Christ. "For I will not venture to speak of anything except what Christ has accomplished through me" (Rom 15:18). Paul has much of which he can boast—and of which he does, indeed, boast: limitless, almost compulsive activity. But in all this, he's the instrument, not the agent. He's that through which God does God's work. Jesus Christ is not a spectator of Paul's ministry, the grateful recipient of Paul's help. When Paul speaks here of his "work for God" (Rom 15:17), he isn't saying that he has somehow done God a good turn by joining the ranks of apostles, lending a hand, putting his weight behind God's case. Paul works *for* God because he is *in* Jesus Christ. He works for God because, over and above his work, God in Jesus Christ is at work, calling and sustaining him as apostle. And so in a real sense it's Jesus Christ who is the agent of Paul's work as apostle; Paul himself is only "minister of Christ Jesus" (Rom 15:16). His work is ministry—that is, a making available, a distribution and setting forth of the benefits of Jesus Christ. Paul's work isn't about him or by him: he's the occasion for the speech and action of God in Christ.

What other service can there be to the gospel? The gospel can only be that to which we're subservient. It's not a commodity for our manipulation; it's not even simply a truth for our preservation. The gospel is an event; it's that event in which the living Christ speaks his word—*his* word, not ours—a word which judges and absolves, cleanses and heals. He speaks. In a real sense, even the apostolic church may not speak the gospel—or at least, it may not do so on its own authority, with its own voice, empowered by its own energy. The apostolic church, like Paul, acts in the power of the Holy Spirit (Rom 15:16). That is, the apostolic church acts insofar as its action is united to that of Jesus Christ. Bound to him, caught up into him, made into his body, and strictly subordinate to him as its head, the apostolic church is a minister of Jesus Christ and his gospel.

Now, the point I want to stress in this connection is this: it's because Jesus Christ is the agent of the church's ministry that the church can relax. Grace chastises us in our anxiety, our sense of omnicompetence and omniresponsibility. One of the most striking features of many of the public statements of churches today is their terribly burdened sense of being responsible—their crushing worry that the truth and trustworthiness and acceptability of the Christian faith rests on the church's shoulders, and that if the gospel is going to survive it's up to us. But such anxious responsibility isn't a sign of the apostolic church.

The apostolic church knows that it's sent to proclaim a gospel that will look after itself. The apostolic community knows that Jesus Christ is alive, unfettered, and omnipotent, striding ahead of us into the world. It's not the church's task to do Jesus Christ's work for him; it's the church's task simply to let him do his work to us and among us and to be the means through which he may choose to do that work. The rest isn't our business. When we do make it our business—when instead of being ministers of the gospel we take it upon ourselves to look after the gospel—then we cease to be apostolic, and thereby we very quickly forfeit joy and peace and hope. Joy and peace and hope in the church are inseparable from believing, and believing—faith in Christ—means freedom. God is God; God will do God's work and will draw us into that work as he chooses. Therefore—relax.

So Jesus Christ is both the origin and the agent of the apostolic ministry of Paul and of the ministry of the apostolic community. Third: What is the content of this apostolic ministry?

In essence, apostolic ministry as Paul thinks of it here is proclaiming or preaching the gospel. Like a prophet, Paul is commissioned to speak. But where the prophet is primarily commissioned to speak to the people of God, Paul's commission turns him to the gentiles. He says he's to proclaim the gospel to the nations, following its unstoppable progress from Palestine to the modern-day Balkans. And his proclamation is part of what Paul thinks of as "the priestly service of the gospel of God" (Rom 15:16); Paul the evangelist is Paul the priest, offering his gentile converts to God as a pure sacrifice, acceptable to God through the Spirit's cleansing power.

But speaking is the key. Not speaking alone, of course, for speaking is accompanied by "signs and wonders"—by the miraculous and drastic working of God in the power of the Holy Spirit

(Rom 15:19). But these deeds have no independent authority to convict and convert. They are there to confirm the word. They aren't in themselves some further kind of proclamation of the gospel, a spectacular but mute and irrational communication of God as a second avenue to the gospel's truth. They're part of that reordering of the world that Christ accomplishes, which break to the surface when the truth of the gospel is announced. But what matters is that they undergird and bolster the apostolic proclamation. They point to the word, and the word points to Jesus Christ himself, the living one who proclaims himself and makes all things new.

Paul is an apostle because he speaks. The church is apostolic because it, too, speaks, because it's a church of the word in two senses. It's a church of the word, first, because it hears the word, lives out of it, is nurtured on it, holds fast to it as the principle of its life, its only hope and salvation. Being this is the basic business of the church and is at the heart of most of the day-to-day struggles of the Christian community. It's a struggle because we can never assume that we are a church of the word. Attending to the word isn't guaranteeable by routine or habit: it has to be won afresh each day. The threats to our life in the word need daily to be resisted; the word needs time and again to be unleashed in our midst.

Second, we hear in order to speak. Public speech about the gospel is close to the heart of the apostolic church's vocation. What makes that public speech difficult are, I believe, two factors. One is that, at least in Britain, we find ourselves in a culture that has largely abandoned public rhetoric as a way of discerning and attending to the truth. We rarely speak, argue, or debate in public: we shout, we sloganize, or we manipulate one another with images. Sadly, even in church life we do that. It's crucial that the church not allow itself to be trapped into compromising with a culture without real words. It's crucial that we insist that there are things that can't be said in five words or two minutes and that those things belong to the world's salvation. We need to recover the vocation of speech, the calling to trustworthy, truthful communication. But there's the second difficulty: the church can only speak what it hears. It can only speak if it knows itself sent. If it loses a vivid sense of its own commission or if it allows that commission to evaporate into a million apparently useful busy tasks, it will end up saying nothing. Or worse, it will end up saying all sorts of things but not say the one thing needful—that the gospel is true; that the testimony of the prophets and apostles is the word of life; that grace is the world's reality.

This may seem a worrisome note on which to end; there is much to be worried about. But grace is more than our worries—it's undefeated. We must wait, and pray, and learn how to listen, and learn how to speak. But we can only do those things if God has mercy on us. And that is why we pray:

> May the Lord grant that we study the heavenly mysteries of his wisdom, making true progress to his glory and our unbuilding. Through Jesus Christ our Lord.
>
> Amen.

CALLED, SENT, AND AUTHORIZED

"AND if any place will not receive you and they will not listen to you, when you leave, shake off the dust that is on your feet as a testimony against them." So they went out and proclaimed that people should repent.

MARK 6:11–12

One of the most striking things about the gospel stories of Jesus is that they present him as one who is always at the center of conflict. His presence, his speech, and his deeds generate opposition. Over the whole of the narrative of Jesus' public ministry are inscribed the words which stand at the beginning of the Gospel of John: "his own received him not" (John 1:11 KJV).

At first, as his ministry opens, Jesus appears as a troubling character, shaking the people of God by an unrelenting insistence on the demands of the covenant and earning the kind of reproaches which fell on the prophets who disturbed the complacency and compromises of Israel. But as we go through the story, we come to see that more is at stake: to encounter him is to encounter a divine summons more immediate, more demanding, more compelling than even that of the prophets precisely because it's the summons of the Lord God himself. In and as this man, the Lord of the covenant himself comes to his people and claims their obedience. And it's precisely that claim which stirs up conflict. They took offense at his healing on the Sabbath, Mark tells us a few verses before the passage that we read—and, as the story continues, we see how offense becomes rejection, and rejection breeds the violence that ends at the cross.

This conflict, moreover, isn't private to Jesus. It envelops all those who find themselves surrounding him, because being in his company involves being precipitated into the midst of God's great dispute with sin. Above all, the conflict extends to those who are called by him to be at the core of all those who assemble around him as his followers—namely, the Twelve, or the apostles. No less than him, they are caught up into the dispute that God has with sin and which finds its focal point in Jesus. No less than him, they're offensive. And no less than him, therefore, they live under the threat of the world's violence. Like the one who sends, the apostolic community itself is inescapably faced with rejection and hostility. And the reason for this is simple: it's *his* community. The stories of the commissioning of the Twelve and the beheading of John the Baptist put before us how the rejection of Jesus is mirrored in the rejection of those whose lives are bound up with him as his witnesses.

What are we to say of these twelve? First of all, and of crucial significance, is this: they are called and sent by Jesus himself. His vocation, his commissioning, and his authorization of them are what make them into what they are. They are apostles. That means, first of all, that they are *called* by him. Their work as apostles doesn't originate in some allegiance which they have to him; its roots don't lie in some decision which they've made—to follow his sheer attractiveness; to join in his protest at the breakdown of the covenant; to seek to express the compassion of God for what is harassed by darkness and death. Nothing in the gospel stories leads us to think that there is any natural affinity between the apostles and Jesus. They're a pure miracle; they're made out of nothing. And so what matters above all, secondly, is *sending*—immediate, authoritative, *making* them into apostles rather than simply crowning some natural sense of vocation. They're called, and as they called they're sent.

All through Mark's Gospel is a twofold movement: a movement toward Jesus in which he seizes hold of human lives and gathers them around himself as the presence of God's salvation, and a movement away from him in which he impels those whom he has called outward. As he impels them outward, he gives them the task of witness: bearing testimony, indicating with amazement the sheer fact of his presence and activity as the one in whom God has arrested the course of the world and bent it back to his purposes. And to do this, lastly, he gives them *authority*. They share in the fact that he has taken charge of human life. They're not powerless. Faced with the forces that seek to destroy the good order of creation and human life, they're not helpless. No! They're the bearers of his authority, acting out of the reality of his sovereignty, having a share in nothing less than the kingdom of God. Apostleship is all this—calling, sending, authorizing by the Lord of the kingdom.

What are they called, sent, and authorized to do? Two things: to preach repentance and to heal. Let me focus on the summons to repentance. The apostles are to preach "that people should repent" (Mark 6:12). They aren't to proclaim some truth of their own devising. They aren't to proclaim themselves. Their proclamation is wholly taken up with what they've heard in Jesus' own proclamation. That is, they're to announce that in the light of the presence of the kingdom of God in Jesus, in view of the fact that God's final rule over all things is being established before their eyes, all stand under an absolute requirement: the requirement of complete and radical reorientation.

Repentance means much more than admission of guilt: it means total redirection, becoming a new person—above all, looking to God and his kingdom as the one truth that alone is to be the center of human life and affection. The apostles don't proclaim simply the need for moral reformation; rather, in proclaiming repentance, they proclaim the need for new birth. And there's an urgency and a finality to this proclamation. The urgency is expressed in the command that they should travel unencumbered, attached to nothing and weighed down by nothing. The finality is expressed in the terrible prophetic sign which they're to give to those who refuse to hear: "shake off the dust that is on your feet as a testimony against them" (Mark 6:11). That is, declare them to be those who have set themselves in opposition to the rule of God, who have heard the summons to repentance but have simply stayed where they are and refused to budge.

Because this is the burden of the apostles' testimony, because they're to testify to God's great interruption of the world in the man Jesus, they're drawn into his conflict. Mark illustrates this conflict in the chapter by turning our attention backward and setting before us the dark story of the death of John the Baptist. On any account, it's a pretty grim tale with a pretty grim cast of characters. Herod: guilty about his marital muddles, like a lot of weak men a prey to superstition, driven by fear, quicker to make an oath than to consider the consequences, a real mess of a man. Herodias: violent, scheming, destructive, her husband's superior in wit and ruthlessness, and not an ounce of fear of God in her. And Herodias' daughter: here, at least, no more than a dancer, the bait to trap Herod—how different from the lovely little portrait of Rachel in Genesis. And John himself. John is the prophet of repentance. He's the one who indicates the coming of the Holy One of God, the arrival of judgment in the person of Jesus.

Herodias is simply affronted, and she wants John dead. Herod's response is more complex. He's both fascinated and repelled. He's fascinated, because he's able to hear in John something of the claim of God. He's repelled, because he knows that really to listen to that claim is to be faced with an unconditional demand that will cut to the quick of his life, which will expose to the scrutiny of God what he seeks to hide at all costs—that his marriage to Herodias is an act of disobedience that accuses him before God. Herodias sees her chance at the party; Herod is trapped by his own promises and becomes the unwilling executioner of the man whom he knew to be righteous and holy.

What's the point of the story? That Jesus is the presence of God; that John is the one who more than any other testifies to the fact that Jesus' coming means divine judgment; and that John's prophetic witness leads to his destruction. And no less than the prophets, the apostles, too, share in the hostility and rejection that is the lot of those who declare the demands of the gospel. What of the church today?

The church is an apostolic community. It can't be said too often that being the apostolic community means a good deal more than having a certain pattern of ordained ministry that we call apostolic. Being apostolic means participating in the same movement that caught up the apostles. That movement, we have seen, is one that involves being called by Jesus, being sent by him, and being authorized by him. The apostolic church is that community in the world that stands beneath this commission, which is defined by it, and which seeks more than anything else to act out this commission.

This means that to be the apostolic church is to be defined by two things: *witness* and *affliction*. The apostolic church—that is, we ourselves —is brought into being by God to witness. It's required to speak the truth of the gospel. Of all other things that are required of the church, this must have preeminence: that it does not keep silence about Jesus Christ but indicates him, points him out, speaks with love and courage about him. And what it says of him is this: he is the one who is the turning point of the world; he is the one before whom and by whom all things are to be judged; he is the one who has made all things new; and, there-fore, repent. To be the apostolic church is to speak the need for repentance. And precisely because the apostolic church is com-missioned to speak that word, it's a church that is no stranger to hostility. If it speaks its word with clarity, the church will pretty soon have to learn how to bear with the rejection and conflict that word generates. To be apostolic is to face the affliction that always accompanies testimony.

All this means that we Christians, if we're indeed an apostolic community, exist within the threats and conflicts of the world. So we face a question: where do things stand with us in these matters? Is our common life as the church of God marked by the affliction that so marked the testimony of the prophets and apostles? If we are indeed marked by that affliction, then the word of the gospel is that, in whatever conflicts we may find ourselves, we're *given authority*. We're given the authority to speak in the name of Christ, even, indeed, to die in the name of Christ. Herod, and Herodias, and all the others, aren't the victors in the world; they're the losers, for they've everything but the one really important thing, which is the gospel, salvation, life, the name of Jesus Christ. If, on the other hand, our common life isn't marked by affliction, then the gospel asks us a question. It asks us whether we're an apostolic community or merely a sort of religious culture. It asks us whether we've fallen into habits which cushion us from the impact of the gospel.

These are matters about which we must each of us examine ourselves. And to help us do so, we may perhaps bear in mind a distinction made by the great 19th-century Danish thinker, Sören Kierkegaard. Toward the end of his life, he wrote an essay in which he contrasted the apostle and the genius. The genius, however exalted, is in the end of worldly reality, and his religion is worldly: it's the refinement of worldly virtue, the studied crafting of the religious spirit. The apostle is quite other: the apostle is called by revelation. At the heart of the apostle is the crashing interruption of God.

Much of church life is, in the end, about the struggle between the genius and the apostle. In that struggle, we can do nothing other than remember this: the community of Jesus Christ is not called to genius; but it is called, sent, and authorized to be an apostolic community, and therein alone lies its well being and its salvation. Amen.

XXVI

PREACH THE WORD

I CHARGE you in the presence of God and of Christ Jesus,
who is to judge the living and the dead, and by his appearing and his kingdom: preach the word; be ready in season
and out of season; reprove, rebuke, and exhort, with complete patience and teaching. For the time is coming when
people will not endure sound teaching, but having itching
ears they will accumulate for themselves teachers to suit
their own passions, and will turn away from listening to
the truth and wander off into myths.

2 TIMOTHY 4:1–4

The church of Jesus Christ is defined by, among other things,
two very basic activities that it undertakes: the activity of
hearing God's word and the activity of speaking God's word. That
is, the church is both a hearing church and a teaching church.

Whatever else the church may do—in its praying and celebration of the sacraments, in its service of the world, in its fellowship
and in its suffering—hearing and speaking, listening to God and
proclamation, are fundamental. Here, we might say, the church is
taken close to the heart of its existence. Hearing and speaking the
word, listening and teaching, are definitive of the church because
in both these activities the church is set in relation to the one great
reality that makes the church into the church: the word of God.
It's through the word that the church was in the beginning brought

into being; it's through the word that the church now is sustained; the church's future is nothing other than the future that is held out to it in the word of God. In short: the church is the *creature of the divine word*, as the thinkers of the Reformation liked to put it. And that creatureliness takes two forms in the common life of the people of God: attentive hearing and astonished speech.

We take the latter first, the speech of the church, that speaking of God's word that makes the church into a teaching church. "Preach the word," Timothy is told (2 Tim 4:2). What is it that Timothy is to preach? What's he to make the matter of his proclamation? The word.

"Word" here is meant in its broader rather than its narrower sense: it refers not so much to the texts of Scripture but very simply to the gospel. The word is the good news of Jesus Christ, the message of salvation at whose center lies the ministry, death, and resurrection of Jesus Christ, and the hope of his return to vindicate his saints. Those events, the great events of God's redemption of the world and his setting aside of sin and death, are a word. That is, they aren't just neutral, flat facts that we can consider from afar, as if they weren't really our concern, as if they did not really impinge on us. On the contrary: they address us. As word they accost us, they come to us as divine communication, they seek us out and set themselves in our midst. And in so doing, they demand of the church a certain kind of *speech*. They demand to be uttered by us also. They make themselves into a matter for our proclamation. And that proclamation is definitive not only of the ministry of the particular character Timothy, to whom this little letter is addressed, but of the church as a whole. Because the word addresses the church, it's to be a church in which voices are lifted up in the speech of proclamation.

Such proclamation is no casual business. It's not the quiet, domestic chat of the community or even the cut and thrust of after-dinner conversation. It is, very simply, *urgent*. It's not restricted in any way by any decisions we might make about what's fitting or convenient; it's not something that on occasion might not be the proper thing to do. "In season and out of season," fashionable or not, Timothy is told, this speech cannot be laid aside (2 Tim 4:2). In this matter, silence will not do, because it's in the proclamation of the word that some things happen in the life of the community that would not otherwise happen.

Proclamation does what isn't done by other instruments: it convinces; it rebukes; it exhorts. It does this because of its relation to the word. The gospel message of salvation convinces—that is, it sets itself in our midst as certainty. The gospel message rebukes—that is, it chastens us in our constant wandering from the reality of God in Jesus Christ. And the same gospel message exhorts—that is, it instructs us in the way of living that is required of us. Because these things are true, then unfailing, patient proclamation is critical: in it, the church is set in relation to its most basic call by being reinvested in the gospel. In the presence of God and of Christ Jesus, Timothy is charged—in the living presence of Jesus Christ, who will appear as judge to assume his kingdom and rule over all things. This is to be the matter of the church's speech.

But if the church is a speaking and teaching church, a church engaged in proclamation, it is only because over and above its speaking, it's a church that hears. Teaching, proclamation, speaking the word, isn't something in which the church takes over God's speaking. The church doesn't speak because God himself has laid aside his own work of speech for a while, retiring to the sidelines and letting the church get on with the job for the interim. No! The church speaks because it is spoken to. Therefore, at the core of its speaking is its hearing, its attention to the word of the gospel. The church does not convince, rebuke, and exhort with its own words but by pointing to the speech of God. Whatever it says is dependent upon what it has heard.

This point is crucial, because it prevents us from thinking about the teaching and proclamation of the church in the wrong way. Teaching and preaching are never anything more than a second move in the life of the church. The first move, the primary reality, is hearing. Only once spoken to does the church proclaim. In my Anglican tradition, this is expressed as the primacy in church of the reading of holy Scripture. It's the lectern that is the primary home of the word of God in church, not the pulpit. It's Scripture read, not Scripture proclaimed, which is the first great act of speech in church. To be the church, to be the community of Jesus Christ that is concerned with the gospel, is first and foremost to listen, to strain our attention toward that word that God himself, present among us as the risen and ascended Christ in the power of the Holy Spirit, now addresses to us in the text of holy Scripture. Here, as always, the fundamental rule: *I heard, and so I speak.*

There is, then, in the church of God, a proper orderly submission to the gospel message in which hearing molds speech and proclamation is grounded in listening. But more needs to be said, and it's this: both speaking and hearing are *threatened.* Speaking and hearing may go wrong. The reason for this is that both speaking and hearing share in the same basic struggle that is true of all reality, the struggle of God against sin. No less than anything else in the life of the community of Jesus Christ, its speech and its listening partake of the dynamic of resistance to God. We refuse to hear. We undertake the wrong sort of speech. And so we oppose the word of God.

What forms does this opposition take? There are, it seems, two very basic modes of this resistance or repudiation of the word. The first, most dramatic and scandalous form, is outright opposition. It's what is referred to here in 2 Timothy as "not enduring sound teaching" (2 Tim 4:3). At its heart, this is a resistance to God that will not bear the content of what the gospel says to us. This resistance is expressed not by being politely deaf but by pushing the word away, by revolt, a kind of adamant refusal to be spoken to in this manner.

In our easygoing ways as tolerant moderns, we tend not to see church life in quite these terms. What earlier generations of Christians might have seen as opposition to the word of God we sometimes think as a sort of benign open-mindedness. But it's worth saying that there is all the difference in the world between on the one hand a genuine diversity of ways of hearing and on the other hand resistance to the gospel, and sometimes what we think of as legitimate diversity may just be a form of opposition to God.

The second form of repudiation of the word is not a matter of revolting against the word but of converting it into something much more amenable to our unregenerate tastes. Rather than being dismissed, the word is reinvented. When this happens in the life of the Christian community, then, 2 Timothy tells us, we get an accumulation of teachers. That is, Christian communities, congregations, collect for themselves those who will say what the community wants to hear. Like a weak leader who has lost his grip and so surrounds himself with flatterers who will soothe his ego and feed him what he wants to know in measured amounts, so the church may be: its hearing is not hearing at all. It doesn't listen to God but talks to itself, and, lo and behold, what it says to itself sounds pretty good. Yet, however pleasing it may be, such hearing and speaking is a death blow—above all because it cuts the church off from that genuine hearing in which alone is its source of life. Once the word is not a judge but a pacifier, then truth has been traded away. The church's hearing is cushioned: it doesn't hit the reality of the gospel like a brick wall. Or as our text puts it: people can "turn away from listening to the truth and wander off into myths" (2 Tim 4:4).

The church's speech is threatened because its hearing is threatened. And its hearing is threatened by lack of hearing, by the primary form of human sin, which is to cease to listen to God and to substitute or supplement what God says with something that God doesn't say. What remedy is there for the situation? How may the church's speech and hearing be secured? Very simply, the remedy is that the church has to take the law of its own existence with absolute seriousness. It's founded by God to be a community which hears the word of God, and so it must hear that word. It's commissioned by God to be a community which speaks the word of God, and so it must speak that word. When hearing is threatened and speech distorted, in other words, the only thing to do is to listen properly and speak well. There's no technique that the church can perform here, no infallible method that will guarantee that once and for all it will get it right. Renewal here is nothing other than a matter of the church being the church, fulfilling its call, holding fast to its commission. But that being said, two further points may be established.

First, hearing and speaking the word of the gospel demand a certain definiteness on the part of the Christian community. They demand, that is, that the church be *this* community, the community of Jesus Christ, and not just any old human community. They require that the church have a certain clarity of profile, a clear shape. In terms of the church's hearing, that means the church will function well when it's much absorbed by listening to its Scripture, looking for the voice of God there, without worrying too much about other voices to which it might attend. There has to be a certain focused intensity in the church's listening: here, not there, we are to expect God's address of us, and so here, not there, is where we will wait. In terms of the church's speech, this means that there will be the same kind of focus. The church will not attempt to say everything but to speak one word and to speak it well. And that word will be the word of the gospel of Jesus Christ.

Second, and last: the church's hearing and speaking are gifts of the Holy Spirit. We're sinners; we don't know how to hear, we have no capacity in ourselves to put the right words in our mouths. Right hearing and right speech aren't within the range of our competence. They're given to us, given by the activity of God's Spirit, in which God opens the ears of the deaf, opens the mouths of the dumb, and makes it possible for us to become true hearers and speakers of God's word. If we hear and speak because the Spirit makes it possible for us to do so, then at the heart of the life of the church, and at the heart of its listening to the Bible and its talk about the Bible, will be prayer: prayer for the coming of God's Spirit, prayer in which the Spirit is invoked because he alone establishes us in the word.

What is the real mark of the church of Jesus Christ? It's that in everything we do—believing, celebrating, praising, interceding, proclaiming, suffering, listening—we make one prayer: *come, Holy Spirit.*

And so we pray:

O heavenly Father, in whom is the fullness of light and wisdom, enlighten our minds by thy Holy Spirit, and give us grace to receive thy Word with reverence and humility, without which no one can understand and speak thy truth; for the sake of Jesus Christ, our Lord.

Amen.

XXVII

WITNESS TO THE RESURRECTION

THIS Jesus God raised up, and of that we all are witnesses.

ACTS 2:32

I want to say a few things about the task of the church to bear witness to the resurrection of Jesus Christ. To come clean from the beginning, what I have to say emerges from a worry to which my mind keeps going back and which I believe these few words from Acts may help us to address. The worry, put simply, is this: one of the biggest threats to the life of the church is a lack of focus.

Perhaps more than anything else, what can eat away at the vitality and persuasiveness of the church's mission is the attempt to be and do and say far too many things, and so fail to be and do and say the one thing that is essential to the church, which only the church can say and which above all things the church must say—namely, that Jesus Christ is risen from the dead, exalted as Lord of all things, the one in whose presence we and the whole world stand. It's the calling of the church of Jesus Christ to make that witness and to do so with constancy, purity, and undeflected attention, and it's part of the church's submission to the discipline of the gospel that it refuses to allow that witness to be crowded out or overlain or pushed aside by all manner of other concerns.

The church can and does set itself a plethora of tasks; all of them can claim to have some legitimate hold upon the church's attention and energy; all of them present themselves with real force to the church's conscience. But unless those claims can make clear that they flow from the task of witness to the resurrection—unless they can show that witness to the resurrection of Jesus Christ will be impaired unless we attend to these matters also—then if the church is wise it will lay them aside and give its mind to one single matter. It will give its mind wholly to Jesus Christ, the crucified, who was raised, who is now at the Father's right hand, and who appoints his church as his witness to bear testimony to him until he comes again in his glory. In the drastic simplicity and purity of that task, the church is to find its calling and to walk on its way.

So much for my worry. How does the New Testament help us to address it? First, there is the overwhelming directness of the core Christian confession: "this Jesus God raised up" (Acts 2:32). What lies at the church's heart, what generates its life and what is to govern its thought and speech and action, is that singular reality: the exaltation of Jesus Christ as Lord.

What is this exaltation all about? Jesus' exaltation at the resurrection means God has ruled out of court one possible way of interpreting the story of Jesus. It would be easy enough to read the story of Jesus as a noble, compelling act of martyrdom, in which Jesus spoke the truth about God and died. To read the story that way would be to say that Jesus shared the fate of all manner of prophets and holy men: he struggled against the world's wickedness; he urged his contemporaries to love righteousness; and he failed, because he was, as Peter puts it, "crucified and killed by the hands of lawless men" (Acts 2:23).

To that way of telling the story of Jesus, the resurrection says, quite simply, "No!" It says that Jesus' fate isn't the same as all other martyrs; he isn't just abandoned to death and waste. No! What looks like just another bit of arbitrary, haphazard history is in fact the outworking of the eternal will of God. The story of Jesus is, in the end, not about his being given over to destruction but about his exaltation. God has raised him up; God has enthroned him; God has made him Lord.

Because his resurrection means that he is Lord, then it isn't simply an extraordinary fact, a curious exception to the finality of death. His resurrection means that he is indeed *raised up*; as the risen one, he shares in the limitlessness of God. He is raised up, and so he shares in God's omnipotence, in God's universal presence, and in God's rule over all things. He, Jesus Christ the risen one, is identical with the power and presence and dominion of God. And if, therefore, we are truly to grasp Jesus' fate, if we are to see who he is, then we are to see this: that in the resurrection, God takes up his cause, vindicates him, and declares him to be Lord.

It's this singular reality, in all its fullness and authority and in its compelling grace, that is the theme of the church's life. It isn't one theme among many; it isn't a truth to be set alongside other truths, as a matter to which, among other things, attention must be paid. This reality, the exaltation of Jesus in which his lordship is acted out before us, is the church's singular and unvarying preoccupation. Why? Because the exaltation of Jesus is at the same time the church's appointment to the task of witness. "Of that we are all witnesses" (Acts 2:32). What governs and directs and empowers the witness of the church is the sheer fact of what Peter calls "that": the raising up of the Son of God through the Father's power to share in the triumph of God.

Now: what are we to say of this witness? First: its origin lies wholly outside of itself. This isn't a task to which the church can appoint itself; it isn't something that the Christian community can take upon itself as a special act of responsibility or commitment. In this matter of witness, the church has no competence or mandate to appoint itself to any task. The witness that is the core of the church is that to which it's called by God alone.

If the church testifies, it isn't because it chooses to speak but because *it cannot but speak* because—despite its inadequacy, unwillingness, hesitancy, and the awkwardness of it all—it must speak. If it's to be itself, it has no option. It can choose to mutter or to gloss over what it has to say with fine words; it can even choose to be silent; but it cannot do those things and be true to its calling.

Second, what the church is called to say about the resurrection is first and foremost simply to point to it as the most real and true and glad thing that there is. Its first task is not to interpret the resurrection, as if the resurrection needed some clever ideas and words to put wheels on it and make it move. Nor is its task to dream up sophisticated arguments for and against the resurrection to satisfy the discriminating mind. Its task is to say, "Here he is! Here is Jesus Christ, unfathomably and insuppressably alive!"

The church's testimony is an act of indication, one great gesture that stretches out towards the risen one and says: he is. How does the church do that? How does the church make that gesture toward the Exalted One? It does so in all sorts of ways; indeed, everything that it does is part of that indication. But there are three particular acts in which the church bears witness to the exalted Christ.

First, the church listens to the risen Christ as he addresses his community in the words of holy Scripture. It submits itself to be ruled by these texts because they're the living voice of the Living One, because in them Jesus Christ speaks in person. And as the church listens in this way, it testifies to the fact that the world is not full of silence or of mere hints and guesses about the truth; it is full of the strong voice of the Son of God.

Second, the church celebrates the sacraments, because they're the acts of the living Christ in which his promises take tangible, visible form: bread and wine to nourish, water to cleanse, the living signs of the Living One's presence and mercy.

And third, the church speaks to the world. It speaks to those who deny or can't be bothered about Jesus' resurrection, and to those who are pleased to think he is dead, and to those who just don't know what to make of it all. And to all of these good folk, skeptics and rebels and the lost and sad and guilty and fearful, the church says the one thing it can say: "this Jesus God raised up" (Acts 2:32).

What, then, is the church's singular preoccupation? Reading the Bible, celebrating the sacraments, and testifying to the gospel. The temptation is to think that this isn't enough: Surely there ought to be more? Well, my suggestion, for what it's worth, is that there is more than enough for the church to do if it does these things, and more than enough to demonstrate the gospel. We don't need to run around fiddling with liturgy, agonizing over what the church's mission might be or packing the gospel into a sound bite for people who think that truth is only 20 seconds long. We don't need to reinvent ourselves. We need to do what the gospel commands us to do: to realize that we're in the presence of the exalted Christ, that the only path open to us is to bear testimony to his presence, and that all other avenues have been closed off.

One last thing: such witness is almost impossible for us, which is probably why we spend a lot of time dreaming up substitutes. It's almost impossible; but what makes it a very real possibility is the fact that the Exalted One himself intervenes to quicken us into his witnesses. He does so in giving to his church the Holy Spirit. In the Gospel of John, the risen one breathes on his disciples and says: "Receive the Holy Spirit" (John 20:22). In giving the Spirit, the exalted Christ empowers his apostles for testimony, sending them as he himself was sent by the Father. And so with us. For good or ill, we are what we are. But we shouldn't forget that part of what we are is an apostolic community, a congregation of those who are sent, and sent for testimony. Such is our calling and our enabling.

May the Exalted One give us grace to make our confession and bear witness to him. Amen.

MESSAGE DELIVERY INDEX

PART V: PROCLAIMING SALVATION

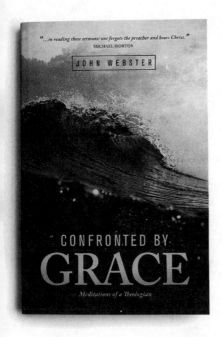